To. Martin.

Cheers!

TARGET ROLLING

A History of Llanbedr Airfield

Wend

Midland Publishing

Contents

Target Rolling
© Jennifer W F Mills, 2002
ISBN 1 85780 136 9

First Published in 2002 by
Midland Publishing
4 Watling Drive, Hinckley
LE10 3EY, England.
Tel: 01455 254 490   Fax: 01455 254 495

Midland Publishing is an imprint of
Ian Allan Publishing Ltd

Printed in England by
Ian Allan Printing Ltd
Riverdene Business Park
Hersham, Surrey, KT12 4RG

Front cover photograph:
A line-up of operational aircraft at Llanbedr,
consisting of Canberra B.2(TT) WK128; Meteor
D16 WK800; Alpha Jet ZJ645; ex-Llanbedr
Hawk T.1 XX154 and new Jindivik Mk 104A
A92-902 (ZJ497). *Peter J Cooper/Falcon Aviation*

Foreword

by Veronica Volkersz
(Llanbedr Staff Pilot, 1957)

Wendy Mills and I have something in common as I was the only woman pilot to serve at Llanbedr in the 20th century and Wendy was the only female target controller. We met in 1991 when she invited me to the celebrations of the 50th anniversary of Llanbedr airfield. I have very happy memories of my time at Llanbedr with congenial colleagues and a great social life.

I was posted there in 1957 to join No.5 CAACU. Employed by Short Brothers, I flew the Mosquito on target towing for the Tonfannau Army Range, which was fairly uneventful, and on fighter control sorties for the RAF.

On the other side of the airfield was the Firefly Drone Flight of the Guided Weapons Trials Wing. In those days this was of a secret nature and operated by the RAF and due to expansion they wanted the airfield to themselves. So my happy times at Llanbedr were shattered when I heard that the Range at Tonfannau was closing and towing would finish at the end of the year. The day I left was one of those clear days when the mountains seemed close enough to touch and the sea had the blue of the Mediterranean. Llanbedr airfield's history is unique and many people will be glad that Wendy has put so much of it on the record.

Veronica Volkersz (deceased)
Cambridgeshire

Preface and Acknowledgements

'That's a pilotless aircraft about to take off,' said my host, pointing at a red and yellow aircraft perched on a strange-looking undercarriage on the runway, attended by men in overalls or white coats.

'You're joking!' said I, but we saw it take off leaving its 'undercarriage' behind on the runway. When it turned seawards a Hawk T.1 roared overhead and joined it. Later the pair returned and we saw there was a skid deployed under the fuselage. The drone made a final approach and landed while the Hawk peeled away. We saw a crane lift the drone back onto its trolley and the combination was towed away. I was intrigued by the operation and wondered who, why and how they had been flying the drone. This was in 1986 as I walked with Kath and John (my weekend hosts) and their dog along the public footpath by the northern boundary of Llanbedr airfield.

For some time I had wanted more interesting flying than my job as a PPL flying instructor/examiner and aviation journalist provided and I scanned the 'Sits Vac' in *Flight International* magazine every week. Soon after my visit to the area a vacancy for a Target Controller at Royal Aerospace Establishment Llanbedr was advertised! Applicants had to be pilots or ex-pilots, preferably with a military background, to form part of a team of five who controlled pilotless target aircraft from the ground; and there were opportunities to fly for those who were interested. Great! I had served in the WRAF too early to fulfil my dream of becoming military aircrew or an airline pilot; but here was a truly interesting job plus the chance to fly again in military aircraft and to be based in beautiful North Wales between mountains and sea. I applied and became a Target Controller until I retired in 2000 at age 65. From the start it was clear that Llanbedr was a centre of excellence for UAV flying, developed over many years by a remarkable group of people and their unusual skills and experiences. What an enthralling business it is!

I dedicate this book, in part, to Veronica Volkersz, the first female pilot at Llanbedr – and the only one in the 20th century, recently deceased. My second dedication is to Maggie Roberts, the first female Air Traffic Controller to be employed at Llanbedr and now the Deputy SATCO. Maggie worked hard to make her dream of escaping from an office and going 'airside' to work come true. I also dedicate this book to those friendly and hospitable Welsh people – past and present airfield staff, colleagues and local residents – who have served Llanbedr airfield with loyalty and affection, and from so many of whom I have received much kindness and encouragement, firstly with *Target* magazine and then with this book.

Here we have a community that is glad and proud to have an airfield close by. Although at the time of writing QinetiQ has no plans beyond June 2004, there is plenty of faith and belief that a longer-term future for Llanbedr airfield will be found.

My final dedication goes 'down under' to fellow Jindivik historians Rob Nash and Ben Dannecker and to all those Aussies and Brits who have crossed and recrossed the Equator to collaborate over the amazing, faithful record-breaking Jindivik. The following poem (printed here by kind permission of Rob Nash) reminds us of how it is in Australia, where the seasons are reversed and the North wind blows hot!

4

Christmas in Australia
by Rob Nash

I know that by now the log fires are burning
And the days when the sun shines unhindered are few
But here it's NOT snowing, the North wind is blowing
And it will be HOT for the next month or two.
The Christmas songs tell us of sleighbells and snowflakes
The radio plays all the old tunes of Yule
But reindeer and Santa all seem so unreal
When you're sipping a drink by the side of the pool
And I can't help but wonder at Christmas 'down under'
And Christmas Eve spent at a barbecue tea
And I think of my kin, where the snow keeps them in
And the frost on the windowpane softens the view
Of a world dressed in white and a long silent night
Round a fire. My thoughts are with you.

Acknowledgements
I am grateful to colleagues from Llanbedr and other units who provided information and photographs, most of whom appear in the book. However, I also owe special thanks to the following: MOD Aberporth, Brian Axworthy, MOD Boscombe Down, John and Caroline Bridgett, Marcus J F Brown, John and Kath Bryant, Dan Carter, Vic Court, Ben Dannecker, Roger Q Davies, Mike Fairfax-Rawlings, MOD Farnborough, Frank Guard, FR Aviation, Bill Hampton, George Hobbs, Basil Jerram, Art Lemon, Neil Lewis, QinetiQ Llanbedr, Jeremy and Cheryl Mills, Tim and Lou Mills, Rob Nash, Serco Operations, Peter W Shaw, Bart Sorge-drager, The Society of Authors, The Spitfire Association, Tony Townshend, Jon Webb, Paul Whitelegg, Derek Whitehead, Glyn Williams, Phil Williams and Paul Wilson.

Wendy Mills   Harlech 2002

About the Author

Wendy Mills joined the WRAF after seeing a recruiting pamphlet that said: 'WRAFs may FLY in service aircraft if they wish.' Trained as a fighter plotter, Wendy spent her off-duty time flying in Tiger Moths, Austers, Harvards, Oxfords, Ansons, Brigands and Meteor Mk 7s. Also, the Air Sea Rescue crews at RAF Horsham St Faith found she was an enthusiastic 'customer' with whom they could practise their winching skills so she spent almost as much time hanging outside their Sycamore helicopters as flying inside them!

Wendy married, completed her service engagement and was 'grounded' as an RAF wife. Six years later she divorced her husband and set about supporting herself and their three children first as a journalist, then as a teacher and then as a flying instructor. By 1979 she was Chief Flying Instructor/Aerodrome Manager of The Sheffield Aero Club and also a CAA Flight, Ground and VHF Radio Telephony Examiner for the Private Pilot's Licence. Wendy continued to write as a freelance for magazines, national newspapers, BBC Radio and Yorkshire TV. At the request of editors she revisited the RAF to fly in and write about the Vulcan, Phantom, Shackleton, Dominie, Jetstream, Jet Provost, Bulldog, Hercules, Hawk, Wessex and Sea King.

In 1987, Wendy was appointed to be the only female Target Controller in the Operations section at Llanbedr airfield and, as one of a crew of five, she flew Jindivik and Meteor pilotless aircraft by remote control. The amount of interest and nostalgic affection for this unusual airfield led her to revive the station magazine *Target* which she compiled, edited and published for the next 12 years. Wendy retired from being a UAV controller in 2000, and this book is the result of her research, interviews and exchanges with the people of Llanbedr airfield from every decade since 1941. She has a daughter, two sons and three grandsons.

The Bards of Llanbedr

I believe that even those readers who may not appreciate the full significance of the following, should obtain much pleasure and amusement from trying to 'read between the lines'.

First Drone Flight by Derek Whitehead

Written within five hours of the first drone flight at Llanbedr in February 1953. 'Sean' is Wg Cdr Sean Scanlon (Ret) and 'Chiefie' is Flt Sgt R M Veitch. The verses were sung to the tune of 'Ar Hyd Y Nos' ('All Through the Night').

In Llanbedr with a Firefly
Red and yellow kite
We can't get the flipping tail down
Oh what a plight

Rain keeps falling, Sean keeps bawling
Everything is quite appalling
If we send it, we might bend it
Let's all sit tight.

It's too risky, mine's a whiskey
Cancel the flight
You're no quitter, mine's a bitter
Let's all get tight.

Suddenly the call was action
Off it went with satisfaction
Rocket missed it by a fraction
Sums can't be right.

Back they came in tight formation
Oh, what a sight
Everyone was at his station
Shaking with fright.

Shepherd, target, what a tangle
Radar spinning like a mangle
Then the deck hook wouldn't dangle
Oh what a plight

With a grumble, Sean pressed RUMBLE
To save the kite
Engine roaring, airspeed soaring
Clawing for height

Four times round and round the circuit
All determined not to shirk it
Till at last said Sean: 'Oh ferk it,
Last one tonight.'

On the deck she came a clanger
With all her might
Heading for the blister hangar
Prospects not bright

Chiefie said: 'It's missed the wires!'
'Swing the sights!' A scream of tyres
Firemen said: 'Oh blast, no fires!'
Turned out alright.

The Azimuth Rider by Dai Bryan

A little story heard this week
About a careless tech man
Who tried his best to be unique
And be a famous stunt man

Caged on top behind a tug
With no one as companion
The little chap felt such a mug
Without communication

While in the front in Rover Six
The couple were so happy
Wendy Craig and Brian Rix
Were towing to their sortie

When at last his plight was known
A fuming tech commander
Became so rude, blue, black and brown
And vanished to his tower.

Glossary of Terms and Abbreviations

ACLS   Air Cushion Landing System.

Acquire, Acquisition   Visual or technical identification of target.

AC2   Aircraftman 2nd Class.

A/D   Assistant Director.

Adj   Adjutant.

AFC   Air Force Cross.

AGS   Advanced Ground System.

Aileron   Control surface for 'rolling' an aircraft around its longitudinal axis.

AMPOR   Aircraft/Missile Proximity Optical Recorder.

AMRAAM   Advanced Medium Range Air-to-Air Missile.

APPROACH   Name of automatic sequence to prepare UAV for landing.

ARMS   Advanced Radar Missile Scorer system.

ASM   Air Speed Monitoring – autopilot function on Meteor drone for maintaining a constant airspeed.

ASRAAM   Advanced Short Range Air-to-Air Missile.

ASR1   Decca Aerial Surveillance Radar, Type 1.

ASTA   Aerospace Technologies of Australia.

AVGAS   Aviation Gasoline.

Azimuth Controller   Controller who steers the UAV by remote control during take-off/landing phases.

Azimuth Trailer   Control vehicle from which a Controller steers the UAV by remote control during the take-off and landing phases.

Banshee   Ground-launched aerial target.

Barrier   Strong mesh device erected on demand across the end of a runway to catch an aircraft that would otherwise overrun.

Bats   Australian term for Azimuth Controller.

Beep   To send a remote control command in pitch or azimuth or the sound associated with these.

Bloodhound (Red Duster)   Early guided missile.

CAA   Civil Aviation Authority.

CAACU   Civilian Anti-Aircraft Co-operation Unit.

CAC   Commonwealth Aircraft Corporation.

CBE   Commander of the (Order of the) British Empire.

CLIMB   Name of automatic system for a UAV to increase altitude.

CRUISE   Name of automatic system for a UAV to maintain a constant height.

DESCEND   Name of automatic system for a UAV to decrease altitude.

DERA   Defence Evaluation and Research Agency.

DESTROY   Name of automatic system to destroy a UAV.

DFC   Distinguished Flying Cross.

DFM   Distinguished Flying Medal.

DRA   Defence Research Agency.

DGTE   Direcorate General of Testing and Evaluation.

Drone   Earlier name for a pilotless aircraft.

DTEO   Defence Test and Evaluation Organisation.

EAS   Equivalent Air Speed.

Elevator   Control surface for 'pitching' an aircraft around its horizontal axis.

Fireflash (Blue Sky)   Early guided missile.

Firestreak (Blue Jay)   Early guided missile.

Firing Box   Clear area within which to conduct a missile firing.

Flaps   Aircraft control surfaces to increase lift/drag.

FRAeS   Fellow of the Royal Aeronautical Society.

GAF   Government Aircraft Factories (Australian).

HUTTS   Hayes Universal Towed Target System.

Hybrid   Air-launched supersonic target.

IR   Infra-Red.

IT6   A section of the Royal Aerospace Establishment's Instrument & Trials Division.

JBRF   Jervis Bay Range Facility.

KCB   Knight Commander of the Bath.

LLHKT   Low Level Height-Keeping Target.

Launch trolley   Three-wheeled steerable trolley for launching Jindivik.

Kalkara   Australian unmanned aerial target.

MANWEB   Merseyside and North Wales Electricity Board.

Master Controller   Senior member of UAV crew with overall responsibility for conduct of UAV sortie.

MEJ   Manned Emulator of Jindivik.

MOD(PE)   Ministry of Defence (Procurement Executive).

MOSART Modulated Output Semi-Active Radar Target.

NAAFI Navy, Army, and Air Force Institutes.

Nav, Navigator Aircrew responsible for navigation of a manned aircraft or Target Controller in Control Cell responsible for directional control of the UAV and operation of certain systems.

NewDERA Government-owned plc born from DERA with PPP.

PAR Precision Approach Radar.

PBX Private Branch Exchange.

PCM Pulse Coded Modulation.

Pilot Australian term for Pitch Controller.

Pitch Controller Target Controller who controls the UAV down the glidepath and lands it by remote control of the elevator and throttle.

Pin Device to hold a Jindivik launch trolley to the runway until ready for take-off.

Pitot (-tube, -head, etc) Part of system for measuring airspeed.

PPP Public Private Partnership.

QinetiQ Name intended for NewDERA after PPP.

RAE Royal Aerospace Establishment or Royal Aircraft Establishment (earlier).

RAN Royal Australian Navy.

Rapier Mobile surface-to-air anti-aircraft missile system.

RPM Revolutions Per Minute.

RPV Remote-Piloted Vehicle.

RTV Rocket Test Vehicle.

Rudder Control surface for 'yawing' an aircraft around its vertical axis.

RVMDI Radar Vector Miss Distance Indicator.

SAMDI Sector Acoustic Miss Distance Indicator.

SART Semi-Active Radar Target.

SATCO Senior Air Traffic Control Officer.

Seawolf Surface-to-air radar-guided missile.

Separation Jindivik release from launch trolley.

Shepherd Pilot and/or aircraft who escorts a UAV.

Sidewinder Air-to-air heat-seeking missile.

'Sights', 'Sight' Abbreviation for Pitch and/or Azimuth Controllers and/or their control positions.

Skid, Landing skid Device on Jindivik lowered for landing in place of an undercarriage.

Skipper Pilot in charge of a manned aircraft or Target Controller in Control Cell responsible for piloting a UAV by remote control and for delegating control or part-control to other crew members.

Skyflash Air-to-air radar-guided missile.

SOS Special Operations Squadron.

Sparrow Medium-range air-to-air missile.

Stiletto Air-launched supersonic target.

Sting Sensor device to initiate automatic sequence on Jindivik touchdown.

STRAIGHT Name of command/system whose functions include cancelling a turn on a UAV.

Stream, Streaming The command or process to trail a decoy target from an aircraft on a length of cable.

Strip Engineer Ground engineer supervising UAV procedures on runway.

Target Aircraft, towed decoy or device at which weapons are aimed/fired or which provides for the practice and/or evaluation of weapons and defensive/counter measures.

TEE Test and Evaluation Establishment.

Telecommand Radio system by which control commands are sent from the ground controllers to an aircraft.

Telemetry Radio system by which information is sent from an aircraft to the ground controllers.

'Thunderbird' (Red Shoes) Early guided missile.

Turnaround The servicing procedure after a sortie that prepares an aircraft or launch trolley for re-use.

Target Controller Earlier name for UAVC.

UAV Unmanned Aerial Vehicle.

UAVC Unmanned Aerial Vehicle Controller.

UDP Universal Drone Pack.

Unstick Become airborne from runway or launch platform.

WRAF Women's Royal Air Force.

WRE Weapons Research Establishment.

WRENS Women's Royal Naval Service.

WRETAR Weapons Research Establishment Target Aircraft Recorder.

Chapter One

'Target Rolling'

'… Cleared take-off … Barrier up … Surface wind one-nine-zero twelve knots … Are you ready, Engineer?'
'Ready to roll, Skipper.'
'On your call, Delta.'
'Clear to select CLIMB.'
'CLIMB on the board, eleven thousand, twelve thousand …'
'Pin gone, Target rolling.'
'Ninety knots … one hundred and ten …'
'Target Rolling, Aberporth.'
'One hundred and thirty … flaps…'
'Airborne'
'One hundred and fifty … seventy … one hundred and ninety …flaps up.'
'In a right-hand climbing turn, Skipper/Nav take control.'
'Radar on target.'
'Nav on target.'
'Select STRAIGHT.'

'Target airborne'.

The pilotless Jindivik jet target climbs rapidly towards Danger Area 201 over Cardigan Bay. The 'Shepherd' aircraft closes into formation. After the pair has levelled the Shepherd observes the streaming of the first decoy tow before leaving the Jindivik to its fate. Back on the runway the orange launch trolley has stopped and the Strip Crew tow it back to the hangar for a speedy turnaround check.

From the moment of 'Target Rolling' until the Jindivik has landed back on the runway, it is flown through remote control by a team of five Unmanned Aerial Vehicle (UAV) Controllers. At the time of the missile firing it is in the hands of the Skipper and the Navigator, seated side by side, in a Control Cell on the ground floor of the Control Tower. The Skipper controls the speed, height, various evasive manoeuvres, selection of transmitter and receiver systems and the delegation of control to others in the team. The Navigator controls the direction, some evasive manoeuvres, operates auxiliary systems and maintains two-way communication with the

Jindivik A92-740 outbound from Llanbedr with two decoy targets, one of which is in the process of being deployed.

Jindivik A92-740 returning to Llanbedr with a damaged tail, burning off flares prior to landing back.

Aberporth Range Controller (40 miles away) who directs the Jindivik flight. Above the hand-operated push-buttons and mini joysticks on the control consoles are VDU screens providing telemetered information from the Jindivik and a television video picture to show the decoy tow.

In the top of the control tower and with overall responsibility for the Jindivik sortie, the 'Master' Controller shares ATC's view of the airfield and visual circuit. He also has VDU and video displays and can take over control if necessary.

There are two 'sight' controllers positioned on the airfield. When the Jindivik is in the circuit pattern they watch it closely through powerful binoculars mounted above their control desks. They wear headsets to exchange information with the Shepherd, ATC and fellow crew members and operate push-button and mini-joystick controls with their hands. The Azimuth Controller, in a control trailer behind the runway threshold, steers the Jindivik during take-off and initial climb-out and then repositions the trailer behind 'the barrier' to face the returning Jindivik and steer it during the approach, touchdown and landing run. The Pitch Controller, in a control cabin abeam the touchdown area, controls the speed, height and attitude of the Jindivik during the final approach and landing.

In a typical operational sortie the Jindivik 'presents' two towed decoy targets, at which the aircrew of two RAF Tornado F.3s each fire an AIM-9 Sidewinder air-to-air-missile in a 'firing box' on Aberporth Range. This area is chosen just before the sortie and is clear of shipping. The 'geometry' is drawn for a planned attack pattern, taking into account speeds, heights, wind and weather. Only if the fighters are correctly positioned are they cleared to fire their missiles.

The targets, streamed behind the Jindivik, are usually destroyed by the AAMs; the Jindivik returns unscathed – or slightly scathed! Sometimes AAMs destroy the Jindivik.

Ex-RAF Tornado navigator John Nichol described this experience in his book *Team Tornado* (Michael Joseph, 1994):

'Before you can fire your missile, there are hundreds of factors that have to be right. There is the Jindivik, a pilotless aircraft that tows the target. There is a Hawk aircraft, that flies alongside you to take still photographs of your missile coming off, and an F.3 that videos the missile firing.

'The next hurdle was to get the Jindivik airborne, and trying to get this remote-piloted thing with two wings into the air is an amazing feat in itself. [Five controllers] actually try to fly this robot around the sky, when just getting it airborne at all is a pretty amazing trick.

'We came in, through the three-minute and two-minute calls..."Where the hell is it?" I screamed, when at last that welcome little blip showed up on the screen...We were closing fast on the target and at 10 miles we turned in to it – until then, we were four miles displaced, simulating a typical attack pattern.

'When you call "Firing", you do not fire the missile and you have to release the transmit button so that the safety people can call: "Stop. Stop. Stop" at any point right up to the death...Finally you call: "Now" and then you pull the trigger, which you have to do with a different hand. "Firing" ... "Firing" ... "NOW!"

'There was the loudest WHOOSH! I have ever heard, as £75,000 of firework came off the side of the aircraft past my left ear. I saw it flashing forward and as I watched it, I made the call of: "STORE AWAAAAAAAAAAY", which unlike "Misfire", means that the missile is off the aircraft.

'I watched the missile streaking across the sky in front of us. It is called a Sidewinder because of the way it moves – just like a snake, weaving from side to side as it homes in on the target. I could see it whacking backwards and forwards until suddenly BOOOM! There was a blinding flash as it hit head-on with the target, and that was it.'

Jon Webb, an ex-RAF QWI and Llanbedr's Officer Commanding Flying described his experience of shooting down a Jindivik:

'As soon as I saw the target I tracked it with the missile-aiming index – known as the "pipper" on many aircraft – all the while listening for the confirmatory "tone" which the missile system generates in the earphones to tell you that it is receiving the infra-red source. I made sure that the detected infra-red source was indeed the target and not

A Hawk T.1A armed with AIM-9 Sidewinder missiles.

reflections of the sun on the sea or from clouds, and that the chase aircraft was not in front of me and that no other factors would render the firing unsafe. You hold the pipper on the target and press the button... There's an almighty silence, especially with the AIM-9G which doesn't come off for seemingly ages. You pray that it won't misfire or that anything else goes wrong. Then it rushes off the rail and smokes towards the target.

'Normally on a line astern attack pattern the missile homes towards the target and detonates harmlessly in close proximity to the decoy target towed behind the Jindivik. However this particular firing was every fighter pilot's dream. The missile carried on past the burning flares that failed to activate the missile's fuse. A split second later there erupted a black and yellow fireball, about 100 feet in diameter, with bits of wing, engine and debris flying out of it in all directions. We passed the codeword to advise that the target had been destroyed and circled the wreckage as it tumbled from 10,000 feet down to the sea. Emotions were mixed; on one hand there was the natural exhilaration any fighter pilot would feel – it was the

first (and only) time I had shot down a full-sized aircraft – coupled with relief that the loss of the Jindivik was not caused by any mistakes on my part.'

Senior Target Controller Dan Carter describes the Skipper's viewpoint:

'Generally when a Jindivik is hit by the missile our computer displays go haywire, jiggling about, lots of warnings flash up and the TV picture goes blank. The Navigator tells Aberporth that we think we've been hit and by this time they can confirm that the Jindivik is destroyed and there's nothing we can do but shut down and come home. However, if it's still flying they'll probably confirm that it's gone into a climb and what level it's passing. If it's still flying we are faced with getting it into level flight and having our Shepherd inspect the damage. If it's practical to return it to base using standard procedure for a non-telemetry approach and landing then we'll do so. But if the Shepherd reports damage that is liable to make it dangerous on the approach to land, then the target is destroyed at sea.

'I can remember one occasion when the Jindivik was hit and we lost all the telemetry. But it was still flying so we levelled off at about 5,000 feet. Then we got the Shepherd joined up to inspect. He reported that the damage was fairly minor apart from one or two holes. So we began the standard procedure for loss of telemetry. But selecting DESCEND and AIRSPEED LOCK put the aircraft into a dive from which it showed no sign of recovery. I beeped it up and selected CRUISE. From then on I avoided the use of AIRSPEED LOCK and flew it manually to circuit height with the Shepherd relaying information on speed and height. HEIGHT LOCK was working so we were able to maintain height and speed above 160 knots. The landing skid was lowered by selecting APPROACH and then going back into CRUISE to get the HEIGHT LOCK in. Then we reduced speed to 150 knots to prove the handling was OK in spite of the damage. We brought the Jindivik back into the Llanbedr circuit with the Shepherd relaying speeds and the Jindivik still in HEIGHT LOCK. When the Navigator turned the aircraft onto Finals I selected APPROACH and we handed it to the Pitch and Azimuth Controllers who made a normal approach and landing but with the Shepherd calling the speeds instead of myself.

Jindivik A92-802 with its centreline landing skid and trailing-edge wing flaps lowered for landing.

'Back in the hangar they found that the airline from the pitot to the autopilot had been severed which suggested an apparent airspeed of zero. This explained why, when I'd selected AIRSPEED LOCK, the aircraft dived trying to achieve lock speed. However on this occasion a successful recovery of the target aircraft was achieved.'

During the 1960s and early 1970s the number of Jindiviks shot down annually sometimes reached double figures, but after a peak of 13 in 1972 the rate fell steadily. By the 1990s the average was 1.3 per year. Missiles and decoy targets were more reliable and the cost of losing a Jindivik was increasing. There were some shootdowns for research or test purposes and sometimes there were technical faults, damage or malfunctions that led to a Jindivik being destroyed at sea for safety reasons. Occasionally Jindiviks were overstressed or broke up during development flights, or they received write-off damage at the hands of controllers on landing. Bringing a damaged Jindivik back to base could produce much adrenalin in the crew! Nowadays, unless everyone is confident of being able to land the pilotless aircraft on Llanbedr's long target runway with its special surface, it has to be destroyed out at sea in a clear area.

Chapter Two

The 1940s

'The early morning train bringing our airfield construction workers from Pwlheli was machine-gunned by German aircraft,' remembered Stella Gumbley. At 18 years of age, Stella saw the momentous change from farming to flying as she cycled around with messages and held measuring tapes for the surveyor.

1941

'I saw the first Spitfire land [at Llanbedr]. We had a good time in spite of the war, with dances and ENSA shows,' said Stella. 'My boyfriend from 131 Squadron recovered radios from crashed aircraft. Once, when he invited me to a dance, he had to work late. A sports car with five mates arrived and they looked after me until he got back from the hills at 11.30pm. Sometimes there were fights because Harlech was full of troops from the regiments training on Morfa Harlech Range and there were so many different nationalities.' On call-up in 1942 Stella joined the Women's Auxiliary Air Force (WAAF), returning to Harlech in 1946 with her Lancaster pilot-husband Derrick.

The new airfield became Royal Air Force Llanbedr on 15th June 1941 and featured two runways of length 3,900 feet (NE/SW) and 3,300 feet (NW/SE). One Bellman and four Blister hangars were also built.

'I was the second pilot to use the new runway after a lost bomber a few days before,' said Christopher Deansley, who landed at Llanbedr in a Boulton Paul Defiant on 1st July 1941. His parents had moved into the family holiday home (a 1904 Boulton and Paul prefabricated bungalow near the airfield) for the duration of the war.

On 20th July Flight Lieutenant Prior became the first Station Commander and elementary flying training in de Havilland Tiger Moths was begun by Airwork Ltd. On 18th August Mr Paul Terry and Squadron Leaders Tanner and Mallinson flew in from Staverton 'to negotiate the use of the airfield by No.6 Air Observer and Navigator School' (ORS (Form 540), RAF Llanbedr, File Air 28/494). On 20th August Wing Commander Barlow continued the negotiations and agreements were speedily reached because the Avro Ansons with their instructors and pupils arrived at Llanbedr a mere four days later!

'We were the first unit at the new Llanbedr airfield,' said Maurice Duberley, then a 17-years-old trainee engine fitter. 'Airwork asked for volunteers to service six Ansons at Llanbedr. As the major servicing was still at Staverton, I got a lot of flying time to and fro. There was always a spare Anson to take people on leave to Staverton and for collecting spares. Once we had six or seven passengers, a bicycle and a dog!'

Civilian ground staff and RAF pilots were billeted at Plas Caemeddig ('The Place of the Doctor') on the mountainside behind Llanbedr village. The local staff included Mrs Thomas, who did the housework, a chef who worked miracles with wartime rations and a lad for errands who was nicknamed 'Enoch'. On the aerodrome itself, Airwork Ltd had a Nissen hut as a workshop and canteen. For the purpose of refuelling aircraft, staff formed a human chain passing four-gallon cans.

One Anson was lost in the first month of training. It was presumed to have crashed in the sea, while returning to Llanbedr from Worthy Down, near Manchester. Flying Officer Shipman was reported missing, believed killed, along with the four others on board. Four weeks later the pilot's body was recovered from the sea off the coast of Anglesey.

'Later we were joined by a squadron of Spitfires who did air-to-sea firing, leaving loads of cannon shells to be picked up from the beach,' remembered Maurice. 'When they left the Spitfires "shot up" the airfield. One of them made a very low pass and crashed near the Officers' Mess, killing the pilot.'

1413812 Corporal G H Booth of the Wirral, a ground gunner, also saw some spectacular crashes. Once a week a Spitfire '... shot the 'drome up for us and we used camera guns to assess our aim. One day I was on the Barmouth to Llanbedr road when the Spitfire's wing-tip hit the water tower of the Officers' Mess! The wing-tip came off; the plane went through some wires and ploughed through trees on the other side of the road.'

The gun posts were sunken metal boxes and spending 24 hours there with snow all around was not easily forgotten. Corporal Booth remembered the armoured car that brought meals out to the gun crews: 'If they took the bends of the peritrack at more than 10mph the car would roll over and our meals were ruined! One night we went stalking rabbits in the sand dunes and got a few with our rifles. The CO was out on the same mission with a shotgun and bellowed at us. We performed the hastiest retreat ever and madly cleaned our rifles. Next morning the regiment was paraded to find the culprits but no one split. We were all confined to barracks for a few nights.'

Early in October, 74 (F) 'Tiger' Squadron's Spitfire IIs arrived, led by Squadron Leader Paul Richey. One aircraft came to grief on landing but the pilot escaped unhurt. Another was lost a few days later when the undercarriage failed to lower and Richey baled out. The squadron's task was to train replacement pilots, help with the defence of Merseyside, carry out convoy patrols and watch over the Irish Sea. This was a 'rest' from intensive operations in south-east England. Aircraft were scrambled to intercept the enemy over the Irish Sea once in October, but made no contact. Flight Lieutenant

P G H Matthews arrived in early November to take over command of 74 Squadron from Squadron Leader Richey who was posted to Fighter Command HQ. Matthews was in action the next day when bombs fell on Holyhead, but the squadron failed to catch the German bombers.

The enemy aircraft took off in France, flew up the Irish Sea taking bearings from the lights of Dublin, carried out high-level bombing raids and escaped across England to Holland for refuelling. Although 74 Squadron's Spitfires repeatedly patrolled and often did dusk patrols right to the Irish coast, their efforts were fruitless until, eventually, one pair intercepted three Junkers Ju 88 bombers over St David's. One of the bombers was shot down, but only Sergeant Ingle returned safely to Llanbedr, his Spitfire covered in oil from the bomber shot down by Williams who failed to return. The pilot's body was recovered from the sea off Pembroke three weeks later.

The social life of RAF Llanbedr began in earnest in November 1941 when 500 people attended the first station dance. However, 'crash landings' and 'forced landings' continued, two sergeant pilots and their aircraft being lost before the end of the year. One was Sergeant A Brown, a Canadian with 74 Squadron, who was practising formation flying and fighter attacks in his Spitfire IIa when he flew into cloud. The Court of Enquiry decided he had lost control and blacked out in a tight turn. His aircraft appeared below cloud at 2,000 feet in a vertical dive, apparently attempting to pull out, but diving into the sea half a mile from Fairbourne. Sergeant C J Stuart, a Scot from Paisley, was killed when, after practising formation flying, his Spitfire crashed and burned out.

1942

In the New Year 74 Squadron was posted to RAF Long Kesh in Northern Ireland. Around 100 of the squadron personnel took the train from Llanbedr Station to embark at Fleetwood for Belfast, while others were flown over in two Handley Page Harrow Transports operated by 271 Squadron. In the middle of their leaving preparations, two sections were scrambled to intercept enemy aircraft over Anglesey without success. Three days later the 13 Spitfires and two Harrow Transports departed RAF Llanbedr.

Early in February 131 (F) Squadron arrived to make Llanbedr their home for three months. Their 14 Spitfire Vs arrived a few days later under the command of Squadron Leader Pedley. The first of the squadron's pilots to be lost after the move was Pilot Officer O'Blenes, who crashed on a return flight from RAF Valley in Spitfire Vb AB242 and was buried in Porthmadog War Graves Cemetery.

Llanbedr's long and historic target service role began in the spring with air-to-air firing practice at drogues, the latter towed by a Miles Martinet. This was laid on for six Hurricanes from RAF Honiley in Warwickshire in late March, led by Squadron Leader Drake. The following day, Short Stirling I N6074/MG-G of 7 Squadron at RAF Oakington was posted missing when it failed to return from bombing the naval dockyards at St Nazaire. When coastguards reported seeing SOS flashes the Pwllheli lifeboat left its moorings at 9.45pm to search east of Celan Head. Then in the early hours of the 26th, an aircraft was reported to have ditched in the sea near Llanbedr airfield. The Pwllheli lifeboat *Minister Anseele* promptly headed for the area while the Barmouth lifeboat *Lawrence Arden* was launched at 0210hrs. The Stirling was floating, hatches open but with no sign of the crew. Come daylight, a rubber dinghy was spotted on the beach. Squadron Leader H L Legh-Smith had ditched after the Stirling ran out of fuel while from the raid. Four of his crew baled out before the aircraft ditched. Then he and two crewmen used the dinghy to reach shore. All seven of the crewmen survived.

Llanbedr staff received an official thank-you for their part in the rescue and the salvaging of the aircraft, the first Stirling to ditch. The Station Commander was promoted and replaced by Squadron Leader E R Bullimore. Later, when the RAF took over the servicing of the Airwork Ansons and de Havilland Rapides, Maurice Duberley joined the RAF and became a flight engineer on Handley Page Halifax bombers.

In May 131 Squadron was 'partied out' and in June 232 (F) Squadron, with Spitfire Vbs, was dined in. All parties, dances and dining-in nights were 'excellent' or 'jolly good'. So when the Senior NCOs beat the Officers at cricket by nine runs, presumably the officers were not dismayed for long as they held their Mess Dance that evening!

Major events in July 1942 were the introduction of a one-way traffic system on the Station, the arrival of the first WAAF, an air raid alarm and an enemy aircraft being shot down by the CO of 456 (RAAF) Squadron in his Bristol Beaufighter. Among the Air Training Corps squadrons to enjoy their 'summer camp' at Llanbedr were those from Rhyl, Llangollen and Anglesey schools. RAF Llanbedr's Form 540, the Operations Records Sheets, notes that during the Station Sports 'in the 100 yds race the Station Commander fell, but failed to break his neck'!

Eight Lockheed P-38F Lightning twin-tailed fighters of the 48th Fighter Squadron, USAAF based at RAF Atcham flew in for one week's air firing practice followed by the 49th Fighter Squadron with 16 P-38Fs. Sadly, one of the aircraft crashed in the sea off Harlech on 27th September. Target services provided by Llanbedr included aerial targets for the fighter squadrons, towed by Westland Lysander TT.IIIAs of the 2025th Gunnery Flight, USAAF; an air-to-ground firing range on Talybont beach and a buoy off the coast for bombing practice. These were augmented by a small naval detachment from 776 Squadron, Fleet Air Arm based at RNAS Speke, with a pair of target-towing Blackburn Skua IIs.

In October three Hurricanes from RAF High Ercall visited Llanbedr for air firing practice, and another four took their turn in mid-December. When 13 USAAF P-38s diverted into Llanbedr due to bad weather, the Mess and anteroom were so overcrowded that it was a relief when they went on their way to North Africa. The Christmas Day variety show demonstrated that 'there was so much WAAF talent on the station'!

Within a few days of their arrival, Yellow Section of 41 (F) Squadron intercepted a Ju 88 east of Dublin and the enemy aircraft took several hits before escaping over Eire.

41(F) Squadron at RAF Llanbedr, 1942.

The year was tragic for 41 (F) Squadron. One week after arriving at Llanbedr, they were detached to Tangmere for the ill-fated Dieppe landings. En route, Flight Sergeant Goodall crashed near Henley-on-Thames and was killed. Then, in the biggest air battle of the war, the squadron lost six pilots including the CO, Squadron Leader G C Hyde. Only five pilots returned to Llanbedr on 19th August. Squadron Leader Tom Neil took command of the squadron, fulfilling his wish to escape from Hurricanes back to Spitfires. However, after two short flights his pride and joy was grounded for an engine change. Afterwards he said: 'I never had the same friendly feeling towards it. Not all Spitfires gave trouble-free service.'

In the autumn three 41 Squadron aircraft went missing after taking off from Llanbedr to carry out formation flying in cloud. Radio contact was lost and 'A' Flight became overdue. Two days later a shepherd found the remains above Dolgoch Waterfalls. The aircraft had descended in cloud and flown into the hillside, killing all three pilots: Flight Lieutenant F N Gillett, Pilot Officer R Harrison and Pilot Officer T R Scott.

Alan Powell of Warton was a 41 Squadron Fitter and kept a diary. On 11th August, two days after recording the departure of planes for Llanbedr, he wrote: 'Up at 0530, left at 7.50am. Pleasant journey via Carlisle, Preston, Warrington, Chester, Bangor, Caernarfon, Porthmadog and Llanbedr at 2030. Good scenery in Wales.' On 14th August again he was up early and reached Tangmere at 2145hrs. His squadron's aircraft flew in on the 16th so Alan was working on them till 2100'.

The next two days he spent 'at work all day working on engine mods till 2130' and then he 'worked on machines till 23.15'. On 19th August he wrote: 'Up at 0300. Breakfast at 0500 and 1030. Dinner at 1430, Tea at 1800. 3 sorties to Dieppe for commando raid. Finished at 2030. CO missing.' On the following day the 'machines left for Llanbedr'; he followed by train and was 'not in bed until 0100.' There were 'Only 3 machines on flight' but on the next day 'new machines arrived'.

On 19th October, with a 48-hour leave pass, Alan received a message that his girlfriend was arriving at Barmouth Station at 1100hrs. He cycled there to meet her, but discovered she was at Bala, NOT Barmouth. His diary recorded the subsequent events: 'Established contact by phone and cycled to Bala. Got there at 1500hrs. When she left Bala I cycled back via the old road. Raining heavily. After tea at the YMCA in Harlech I arrived at camp at 2000, very wet.' On the 22nd he wrote: 'Three A Flight machines missing. Issued with cycles.' (He had previously used his own, brought from home). Two days later: 'Three A Flight pilots found crashed on hillside.'

Alan noted that, 'During 64 months in the RAF I moved some 50 times; many were stops of short duration. The exception was Llanbedr and I look back on it with fondness.' Just before leaving Llanbedr, Alan wrote: 'Afternoon off. Cycle ride among hills beyond Harlech. Saw first lambs.'

1943

It was tempting fate to log 'another month without a prang' in January! On 1st February Sergeant Barnaz died on crashing at Pwllheli, apparently during unauthorised low flying. After traditional farewell celebrations at the end of February, 41 Squadron departed for High Ercall in Shropshire. In March a sea search by aircraft from Llanbedr and Valley found Lieutenant Lilley of the 2025th Gunnery Flight, USAAF, after he had baled out of his Lysander south of Bardsey. The body of his winch operator was eventually washed up on Barmouth beach.

Llanbedr's role changed from Fighter Station to No.12 Fighter Gunnery School in 1943. The targets were drogues towed by Martinets over Cardigan Bay; ground targets on the beach at Talybont Range or sea targets anchored off shore. In four days of air gunnery practice, seven American Republic P-47 Thunderbolts from RAF King's Cliffe in Northamptonshire fired some 12,980 rounds, scoring 355 strikes on the drogues. However the RAF were more impressed by the Americans' baseball games and commented that the barracking was as interesting as the game! It was noted that 'USAAF aircraft, pilots and ground crew will shortly be leaving. Whilst at RAF Llanbedr their manners and attitude to the RAF were above reproach. They won our deep respect and affection'.

After repainting No.1 Dining Hall, Llanbedr was attempting to win the Fighter Command Dining Hall Contest, so 13 USAAF Spitfires from Monbury that refuelled at Llanbedr earlier, flew back to Llanbedr for lunch! Fortunately the Catering Officer 'always finds the necessary extra rations when guests arrive unexpectedly!'

The strength of the station was 20 RAF and two WAAF officers and 123 other ranks. Officers and senior NCOs wanted to ease their manpower problems by using POWs, but found this wasn't permitted under the Geneva Convention. So visiting pilots were conveyed to the Mess in a pony and trap. One night the din in the Mess was so loud that the waiting Station pony and trap fled but were later found unhurt on a dispersal site.

When 1533 Flight from Colwyn Bay County School's ATC squadron arrived at Llanbedr for summer camp, teenager schoolboy Eddie Doylerush was among them: 'The Mosquitoes and Beaufighters took it in turns to dive and shoot up targets on the beach. Although I was keen on collecting aircraft serials and code letters, I did not wish to be taken for a spy, so just made a mental note of the code on one "Mossie" – RO-P. Our Flight Sergeant, Hesketh Hughes, was given a flight in a Mosquito and we marvelled as it zoomed around. When it landed we rushed up and I've never seen anyone look so green! As a result there were no more takers for a flip and I always regretted not going.'

During their week at Llanbedr the boys took turns on the Link trainer, as Eddie recalled: 'I managed to hold it on a straight course and had a commendation from the instructor. I didn't tell him that in the shed at home I had made a mock-up of a cockpit complete with instruments "rescued" from non-fatal crashes.' Later on, Eddie flew in a Halifax and Ansons and attended the gliding school at Tal-y-Cafn in Conway Valley. Later in his life, while climbing in Snowdonia, he came across the wreckage of an Anson, one of the aircraft types in which he'd flown. After trekking to many other crash sites he was amazed to learn how many survivors there were from aircraft crashes in the mountains and he became an aviation researcher and the author of four books on the aviation history of North Wales, relating many of the stories behind aircraft crashes and the birth of the RAF Mountain Rescue Service.

On 15th July a female pilot of the Air Transport Auxiliary (First Officer Blackwell) landed from RAF Hendon and departed later for her base at White Waltham. Then the 'flying Dutchmen' arrived at Llanbedr.

Formed at Woodvale on Merseyside in June 1943, 322 (Dutch) Squadron was comprised mainly of Dutch pilots and was among the first of the RAF fighter squadrons to fly into Llanbedr for armament practice camps of seven to ten days' duration, in preparation for D-Day. However, when Flying Officer Muller paid a visit to Llanbedr his Spitfire was blown into the boundary fence. The aircraft was badly damaged but Muller was unhurt. Six more 322 Squadron Spitfires along with the CO, Squadron Leader Stewart, flew in to be ready for operations at 0515hrs the following morning.

Author's Note: In 1993 we saw a man 'acting suspiciously' outside the perimeter fence as we prepared to land a Jindivik. Security guards escorted him away but months later I had the pleasure of escorting him (Amsterdam photographer Bart Sorgedrager) on a more official visit, to obtain the photographs he attempted to take on his unofficial visit! They were for a book commemorating 322 Squadron's fiftieth anniversary for which he was collaborating with Drs W H Lutgert, fellow researcher at the Air Force History Section of the Royal Netherlands Air Force. Bart had a special interest because one of his uncles, Bert Wolters, fled from Holland to England to help in the fight against the Germans and served as a pilot with 322 Squadron until he was killed on 16th September 1944 when his Spitfire IX (MJ460) crashed after a mid-air collision while on an armed recce to Holland. Bart never knew his uncle but 'in special homage' to him decided to make a photographic history of 322 Squadron.

Personnel of 322 (Dutch) Squadron while at Llanbedr, 1943.

When the Spitfires departed four Mosquitoes arrived to carry out air-to-air firing the following day (in conjunction with two Beaufighters) with 1486 (Fighter) Gunnery Flight. On 23rd July all the aircrew were reminded by the Station Commander of Air Ministry orders regarding 'Low Flying Offences'. On 27th July a total of 34 air-to-air firing sorties was achieved and the air-to-air firing practice activity increased throughout the rest of the year. In the early hours of 4th August, Boeing B-17F Flying Fortress 42-3124 *Mr Five by Five* of the 427th Bomb Squadron, 303rd Bomb Group (Heavy) – the 'Hell's Angels' – crashed into the western side of Arenig Fawr, near Bala, while on a cross-country navigation training flight. The Home Guard and RAF Llanbedr's medical officer responded but the eight airmen had all been killed. Later in the day, Major Hagenbach of the 303rd BG flew to Llanbedr from the unit's base at Molesworth, in another B-17F, to assess the crash site.

In the middle of the month the Station Commander, Squadron Leader Bullimore handed over to Squadron Leader Sutton DFC The new CO, nicknamed 'Scruffy', was a New Zealander who had lost an arm. On 8th September he announced: 'Italy has accepted surrender terms'. Pilot John Sutton (no relation) said that being offered a lift in Scruffy's Hillman Minx was 'hairy because the CO would leave go of the wheel to change gear during which operation the car would swing violently!'

John Sutton had a 'hairy' sortie when he levelled out at 800 feet to stream a target drogue and an ear-splitting noise was accompanied by tremendous vibration. His Geordie crewman apparently shouted 'Fire!' and there was a smell of over-heating. John dived his aircraft for the deck but then all went quiet again. 'We had winch brake failure and it was the speed of the cable loss off the drum that caused the smell, vibration and noise. Geordie had shouted "Wire" not "Fire"! I treated the job more seriously from then!'

John's philosophy of life was that there always seemed to be a funny side. He said the WAAFs were the mainstay of the Signals, MT and Safety Equipment sections, and 'God knows how we would have got by if Thelma, our driver, had ever reported Sick!'

Personnel of 12 Armament Practice Camp gathered around the tail of a Westland Lysander TT.III. Leading Aircraftman Haywood is at front left.

John felt a deep affection for the Welsh, their country and the local people who helped in times of stress:

'We relied on Mr Warburton, landlord of The Vic with its six-day licence for our early evening drinking. Ex-butcher Will Pugh provided a taxi service and I once counted 16 airmen of all ranks travelling in or on Will's Austin. Most squeezed inside while two hung onto the nearside window with their feet on the running board and one sat perilously on the pull-down luggage rack at the back, and all for a shilling a head. No matter where you were – Harlech after the cinema, Dyffryn at 'Ma Griff's' restaurant, Barmouth on return from leave, sober or skinned up – Will was at readiness! Mr Jack Workman, who farmed Mochras would also give a lift if he happened to be in the Mess when one was needed. Harry Jones, the railway guard took bets and Mr ...., the poacher also rendered valuable services!'

In October 1943, 1486 (Fighter) Gunnery Flight was reformed as No.12 Armament Practice Camp with Miles Masters and Martinets

Two group photographs of personnel assigned to 12 Armament Practice Camp.

and Westland Lysanders. A member of 12 Armament Practice Camp was Leading Aircraftman Arthur B Haywood, a fitter whose wife and daughter sometimes came by train and stayed in the Llanbedr butcher's shop. His daughter Audrey recalled how she and her mother 'walked down to the aerodrome to see Daddy or he would join us in Llanbedr when off duty. My father's diary has payday entries, e.g. £3.12s'.

Two days later, three P-47s from Hatfield arrived for air firing practice and two more arrived on 3rd November. On this day Harry A George was particularly grateful for Llanbedr airfield. He was the co-pilot of a 26 OTU Wellington X (HE872) over the Welsh mountains and remembered all too well the subsequent events:

'At 16,000 feet we flew into cumulo-nimbus cloud and all of a sudden everything went haywire. I was pinned to the top of the aircraft by the forces that took control of us as the aircraft started a steep dive. This became so steep that everything loose hurtled to the nose. There was terrific noise from the engines as we careered down, still in cloud. Les Edwards, the Skipper, and I pulled back on the stick, to no avail at first. But gradually the rate of descent became more controlled and we broke cloud over the water with the aircraft still refusing to maintain height. We said: "Just ditch it, Les!"

'But then a runway appeared and we were perfectly lined up for it. So we "arrived" at Llanbedr! Next day, Les took Wellington 872 for an air test. "Chick" Chigwidden, our RAAF navigator, and myself did not go on this ill-fated flight. The aircraft crashed into the hill at the end of the runway. Les was injured, so we did not fly together again as a crew. Our rear gunner, Sergeant N O'Hamley, sustained head injuries and Sergeant Humpage, our poor old mid-upper gunner, was killed.'

The record states there was 'good work' by the Station's fire and medical teams who reached the scene of the accident speedily. Eirian Williams remembered seeing the remains of the crash on their land when she married Ewart after the war and went to live at his farm adjoining the airfield. 'The Wellington had missed the haystacks and

the farm by about 200 yards and flattened one wall. We kept finding bits of wreckage, also shells from when the pilots used to fly down Cors-y-gedol Drive and shoot up targets on the beach and in the sea. I saw one plane crash into the sea – sadly the young Canadian pilot was killed. There was a Defiant that crashed into the water and if the tide had been out the two would not have drowned – they were so near. And I saw a plane come down on the sand dunes but the pilot had parachuted out, so he was OK.'

From a local farming family, Eirian was exempted from military service, but 'I was always fascinated by the aerodrome and used to go to the dances. Before the long runway was built the flight path came over the farmhouse and those twin-fuselage aircraft [P-38 Lightnings] skimming low made our baby John duck in his pram. Nowadays the aircraft don't bother me, but I still look out of the window and watch what's going on.'

Douglas G I Macdonald was in charge of signals at 12 Armament Practice Camp. Miles Masters and Martinets were crewed by a pilot and drogue operator who flew out into Cardigan Bay and winched out a white cloth drogue behind the aircraft. They towed this up and down while the visiting operational fighter squadron aircraft fired at it. The ammunition was coated in a special paint of a colour unique to each aircraft. A shell passing through the drogue would leave a trace of paint around the hole and afterwards it was easy to count the holes colour by colour and proclaim the result.

In mid-November 322 Squadron returned with 14 Spitfire Vs for air firing practice and 13 Armament Practice Camp arrived with their towing aircraft, followed by their Commanding Officer, Squadron Leader Crafts. At an Officers' Mess Dance it was recorded that the Dutch aircrew 'can sing, but not dance!' Two more 322 Squadron Spitfires suffered taxying accidents and Flight Lieutenant Plensman took off for Woodvale but 'crash landed three miles from Newquay in South Wales.'

No less than 32 Spitfire Vs arrived at the beginning of December, with only one mishap – a belly landing. These aircraft were from 310 and 312 (Czechoslovak) Squadrons from RAF Ibsley in Hampshire. They achieved 349 air-to-air and air-to-ground firing sorties during their Armament Practice Camp. Then 29 Spitfire Vbs of 306 and 315 (Polish) Squadrons flew in from RAF Heston, Greater London. After the usual Christmas Dinner, Dance, church services and Concert Party Revue, the Poles achieved 214 air-firing sorties with the loss of one aircraft that crashed near Aberystwyth and a collision between two taxying Spitfires.

1944

The Poles departed on New Year's Day and then 331 and 332 (Norwegian) Squadrons arrived with their Spitfire IXs. After their Air Gunnery practice at Llanbedr the Norwegians shot down four enemy aircraft on their very first sweep! Next came the Mustang IAs of 168 Squadron from North Weald and then 504 Squadron from RAF Hornchurch in Greater London, with Spitfire IXbs. In early February when 504 Squadron left, it was the turn of 268 Squadron's Mustang Is from North Weald and 350 (Belgian) Squadron's Spitfire IXs from Hornchurch. Phyllis Parker, remembering her service at Llanbedr as WAAF 480217 Phyllis Smith, recalled those days: 'The place was so alive and the visiting pilots so full of enthusiasm for the joys of flying. It was called a "rest cure" but it wasn't at all restful and there were many different nationalities. The ground crews came with them and slept under canvas. We only had a skeleton permanent staff then.

Our one-armed CO brought his plane down on the sands behind Flying Control. His WAAF driver was very surprised when he asked her to fetch his arm from the seat of the plane! He lived with his wife and baby daughter, Vicky, in a house on stilts near the camp. It must have belonged to someone who loved boats because, when I was baby-sitting, I noticed that all the carpets and cushions were blue with white anchors.'

Phyllis was a cine operator and one day after flying had finished she left Flying Control to cycle round the perimeter track carrying a film. Suddenly two Spitfires appeared and she was blown off her bicycle and the film blown out of her hands! She celebrated her 22nd birthday at 'Ma Griff's', an occasion she recalled after revisiting the airfield in 1999: 'As well as the usual meal of ham, egg and chips (a luxury at that time because only the aircrew were normally given real eggs) I was given a sponge cake and a bunch of lilies of the valley – the flowers for a May birthday. It was certainly one to remember!'

In February two aircrew were killed when a Mosquito crashed in the mountains and a Beaufort went into the sea off Barmouth after the pilot baled out over land. Mustangs continued to make use of Llanbedr during the early months of 1944 when 268 Squadron from RAF North Weald arrived with their Mustang IAs. Also making the journey from Hornchurch were the Spitfire IXbs of 350 (Belgian) Squadron and the Spitfire LF.IXbs of 66 Squadron, while 317 (Polish) and 340 (Free French) Squadrons arrived with their Spitfires from Northolt and Merston. All completed Armament Practice Camps at Llanbedr, as Andrew Deytrikh of 66 Squadron remembered: 'We learned the art of dive-bombing with small smoke bombs at Llanbedr. We were fed like fighting cocks;

WAAF Phyllis Smith.

there appeared to be no such thing as food rationing. It was great fun and I enjoyed every minute of it. Later we were armed with 500lb bombs which we dropped on German radar sites on the north coast of France.'

There was a Leap Year Dance, football and rugger matches (the Royal Marines beat the RAF at both), an ENSA show and a visiting Band Concert.

Corporal Fitter Bryan Stone served in 'D' Flight of No.3208 RAF Servicing Commando and was detached from his base at RAF Ford to service 66 Squadron aircraft at Llanbedr between 21st February and 8th March. During this time he had a dreadful insight into a tragic accident '… that has come back to me many times over the years. A Spitfire landed after carrying out an air attack on a ground target. The pilot climbed out looking as white as a sheet and said in a very strong accent: "I think I have killed someone. My radio was not working." Apparently a young Irish airman had walked onto the ground target as the pilot started his firing exercise. He only fired 20 rounds from each gun, but it was more than enough to kill the poor chap.'

The accidental shooting of Leading Aircraftman Wright on Dyffryn air-to-ground firing range on 4th March was followed by a Coroner's Inquest on 6th March and a Requiem Mass at Barmouth Roman Catholic Church on 13th March. Then 602 Squadron's Spitfire IXs arrived at Llanbedr to experiment with 500lb bombs and there was a second fatality on the Dyffryn Range when Flying Officer Hale crashed. 'Spit-bombing' began in various theatres of operations during World War Two as resourceful units devised ways of using 250lb and 500lb bombs – and there was at least one attempt with a 1,000 pounder! At Llanbedr in 1944, Pierre Clostermann was among the pilots involved in developing and refining techniques to enable Spitfires to dive-bomb German V-1 launch sites with 500lb bombs. He wrote about this work in *The Big Show* (Chatto & Windus, 1963): 'Dive-bombing with Spitfires is a technique on its own, as the bomb is fixed under the belly of the machine, in the place of the auxiliary tank. If you bomb vertically the propeller is torn off by the bomb. If you bomb at 45° aiming is very difficult.'

However, by trial and error 602 Squadron evolved their technique and visiting VIPs from Inter-Allied GHQ watched with great interest. The squadron began at 12,000 feet in close reversed echelon formation. When the leader sighted the target under the trailing edge of his wings he dived at 75° with full throttle. At 3,000 feet they started pulling out, counted to three and let go the bomb. On one trial the bomb from one Spitfire hit another Spitfire, flying at 450mph, but the pilot baled out. Once a bomb 'hung up', then came free as the pilot made a low pass to signal his intention to land with the bomb still attached. The explosion in the middle of the airfield covered the VIPs with mud! The dive-bombing technique also surprised the Germans when used successfully against V-1 installations at Bouillancourt and Ligercourt.

While the Royal Navy (HMS *Glendower*) beat the RAF Llanbedr football team, the WAAFs beat the WRENS at hockey. The WAAFs also found time to organise a weekly dance in addition to the frequent Mess and Squadron parties and ENSA shows. During March the two Armament Practice Camps logged the Spitfires of 302 (Polish) and 308 (Polish) Squadrons, both from RAF Northolt, and the Spitfires of 602 Squadron from RAF Detling in Kent. More Spitfires arrived from RAF Hornchurch courtesy of 485 (NZ) Squadron; and 306 (Polish) and 315 (Polish) Squadrons, both transitioning from Spitfire Vbs to Mustang IIIs, made the trip from RAF Heston. Max Collett, from Napier, New Zealand, then of 485 (NZ) Squadron, remembered his squadron's deployment to Llanbedr: 'To set the record straight: we were flying Spitfire Mk IXs while at Llanbedr, not Typhoons, thank goodness. Our squadron did fly Typhoons for a short time and we were not impressed when comparing them to the Spitfire.'

Max Collett recorded 485 (NZ) Squadron's deployment in his Squadron Operations Record Book: 'The Squadron was detailed to attend No.12 Armament Practice Camp, Llanbedr, from 21.3.44 to 27.3.44 for the purpose of practice bombing and ground strafing. No.5 Daily Servicing Section of No.135 Airfield accompanied the Squadron on this exercise. During this week 135 sorties

Top: **66 Squadron: Dizzy Allen, CO of the Dive-Bombing School (seated 4th from left); Andrew Deytrikh (seated 3rd from right).**

Above: **485 (NZ) Squadron; Max Collett is 2nd from right.**

were flown although the Squadron was unable, through weather conditions, to reach Llanbedr before 1100hrs on 24.3.44. Had to leave early again on the morning of 27.3.44 to return to Hornchurch to partake in Exercise Lambourne which commenced on 28.3.44.'

April began with a fatality when a convoy of jeeps and lorries from No.135 Airfield left for RAF Coolham in West Sussex and four lorries overturned outside Dolgellau resulting in injuries to several airmen and the death of AC Swiatezak. WAAF Phyllis Smith had caught a lift with this convoy to spend her day off in Barmouth. Then she noticed motorcycles and ambulances busy on the road back to Llanbedr. 'I had to report to the Guardroom when I returned to the Camp by train because they knew I had started out with the convoy and they wanted to check if I was alright.' Following a Coroner's Inquest on the dead airman, he was buried in the Military Cemetery at Porthmadog.

On 8th April a Summary of Evidence was taken against Flight Sergeant Stratford and Sergeant Tryner for being out of bounds on the WAAF site! Two days later No.136 Airfield arrived and demonstrated their mobility skills by NOT requiring Station facilities. The airfield altered overnight with the arrival of all their vehicles, tents and mobile kitchens but resourcefulness went too far when two of their airmen were caught trying to steal a Hillman car.

'Some weeks before D-Day a target was set up in the sea off Dyffryn and visiting rocket-firing squadrons tested their prowess,' remembered Douglas Macdonald who explained that as each rocket landed on or near the target, bearings were taken from land and the results plotted. 'Llanbedr was a station to which most air force personnel quickly became attached. The village was small so you soon became familiar with buildings and residents. In the Victoria Inn by 8pm it was impossible to see across the saloon and lounge due to the cigarette smoke. Females started to patronise the pubs and the WAAFs led the way. Their presence in "The Vic" caused raised eyebrows among some local residents who contended that after closing time (at 9pm) there were far too many "goings on" in the village!'

There were no 'goings on' at 'Ma Griff's'. Serving the boys in blue with an appetising meal that they could afford was her personal war effort. Provided her customers were well-behaved, 'Ma Griff' was charming but when she overheard someone making a comment on the size of his portion of chips, she threatened him with a saucepan. 'My colleague ate up and shut up as instructed and on future visits made sure to speak kindly of "Ma Griff's" generosity and culinary expertise. And, to be fair, "Ma Griff" always welcomed back those who had previously upset her,' recalled Douglas Macdonald.

Douglas also recalled the Dyffryn policeman who hid in the shadows, suddenly emerging to apprehend RAF personnel cycling to Barmouth or to 'Ma Griff's' without lights. (Cowled lights that were not visible from the air were compulsory.) Then he issued cautions with a twinkle in his eye. When he stopped a four-seat taxi with seven airmen and WAAFs inside and an airman clinging to the boot, all singing a coarse version of 'She'll be coming round the mountain when she comes,' he again cautioned the unruly party and waved it on, although windows and doors were being opened as the local residents sought the origin of the din.

'The girls who worked in the corner café opposite The Victoria helped to ensure our custom for tea and cakes to supplement the air force lunch,' added Douglas. 'There was "Llanbedr Lu", a youngish lady with a glad eye for anyone in blue. The more senior the rank, the gladder her eye! The NAAFI and the Station cinema were near the dining halls on what became the Maes Artro tourist village; and it was a Polish pilot who flew under the bridge at Barmouth!'

The formidable Hawker Typhoon arrived at Llanbedr when 349 (Belgian) Squadron from RAF Coolham and 193, 164 and 183 Squadrons from RAF Thorney Island in Hampshire attended Armament Practice Camps at Llanbedr. Flying Officer Broadhurst was lost when his Typhoon crashed into the sea off Dyffryn, the wreckage washing ashore a few days later. Broadhurst began his dive at 10,000 feet and fired his rockets on passing through 5,000 feet but pulling out too sharply the aircraft did a high-speed stall, flicked over and spun inverted into the sea. April 1944 ended with RAF Llanbedr playing the last match of the football season against HMS *Glendower* and the first match of the cricket season against RAF Llandwrog.

In May Nos 340 and 341 (Free French) Squadrons from Merston in West Sussex flew in for Armament Practice Camps. The latter squadron lost a Spitfire IXb when it caught fire in the air but the pilot baled out and was unhurt. The Station Commander's Miles Magister was 'written off' on ditching, following engine failure, after take-off. He and his passenger were rescued unhurt. William Jenkinson, a flight mechanic with No.13 Armament Practice Camp, described the incident: ' "Scruffy" Sutton took off with a young co-pilot, who left the mixture control in "weak" so the aircraft dropped in the sea off Mochras Island. We were detailed to drag the Magister ashore across the rocks from where the RNLI had towed it.'

RAF Llanbedr received a congratulatory message from Air Chief Marshal Sir Trafford Leigh-Mallory KCB DSO, Air Commander of the Allied Air Expeditionary Force, for the work done by Nos 12 and 13 Armament Practice Camps at Llanbedr. Then, soon after D-Day came the announcement that they would be closed down. In July eight ATA pilots were flown in to collect eight Martinets. The five Sergeant pilots who had been towing the drogues were posted to OTUs and all the remaining aircraft were flown away, the only exception being the Station Commander's replacement Magister.

On 8th September an event took place that held deep significance for the future of Llanbedr airfield. This was a mysterious explosion in Chiswick, followed by a sonic boom. Then there was another explosion and another sonic boom, this time in Epping. These were different from the thousands of V1 pilotless flying bombs that announced their arrival with loud pulsating jet engines that suddenly stopped, leaving a short eerie silence as they dived until the warhead detonated. The difference was that the Germans had launched their first A-4 (V2) rockets at London from The Hague. The rocket could be launched from a mobile unit and could carry a tonne of high explosive to a target over 190 miles away. Guided by an autopilot, it was propelled above the atmosphere before free-falling along its trajectory at supersonic speed. In the following six months London was bombarded by V2s until the Allies drove the Germans from Holland.

At Llanbedr and in the near vicinity there was a depressing record of aircraft mishaps and crashes. The bodies of Flight Sergeant Waring (NZ) from RAF Westcott in Oxfordshire, Sergeant van Every and Pilot Officer Watson from RAF Peplow in Shropshire and Flight Sergeant Gray were washed up on different days during the summer. On the night of 30th August Halifax V LL283 of 1664 Heavy Conversion Unit at RAF Dishforth crashed three miles northwest of Porthmadog while on a cross-country training flight, with the loss of two of the eight-man crew. On the

base itself a USAAF B-17 overshot the runway and sustained slight damage, followed by an RAF Wellington, but thankfully none of the aircrew were injured in either of the last two 'prangs'.

Less fortunate was Flight Officer Peter Quinci, killed when his P-47C Thunderbolt of the 495th Fighter Training Group crashed on Aran Mawddwy on 16th September while on a training flight. The wreckage and Quinci's body were not located until 22nd September. A B-25 Mitchell sustained prop damage while taxying at Llanbedr and another Mitchell flew in with the required spares next day. Next, a Halifax landed with instrument failure and was collected by a pilot flown in aboard an Anson. Additional aircraft diverted into Llanbedr during bad weather and 'flying boot containing foot and part of leg washed up on Mochras island' was the last sad entry in the Station Diary for 1944.

1945

The early log entries for this year covered the crash in the Rhinog mountains of Lancaster III NE132 from 1653 HCU at North Luffenham in Rutland after breaking up in cumulo-nimbus cloud on 6th February. The pilot stayed at the controls while two baled out, but they were too low and all seven of the crew died. Mosquito FB.VI NT221 crashed after a fire in the air and the pilot, Flying Officer Roberts DFC, died in Porthmadog Hospital two days later. A Beaufighter TF.X from No.1 Ferry Unit at Pershore was found three weeks after flying into Aran Fawddwy summit on 10th February while on a fuel consumption test, the bodies of pilot Flying Officer A L Roe, RAAF, and Warrant Officer Newbry being recovered with great difficulty. Flight Lieutenant Roberts belly-landed his 631 Squadron Vultee Vengeance IV when the squadron moved from neighbouring Towyn to Llanbedr in May 1945 to fulfil an army co-operation role until 1949 with Vengeances, Hurricanes and Martinets.

Pilot John Sutton remembered the arrival of 631 Squadron at Llanbedr: 'Then Squadron Leader Joe Pegg turned up with the rest of 631. The Adj was Flying Officer Bob Warr. One of their Flying Officers weighed in at about 14 stones and did serious ballet dancing across the Mess. Joe, no lightweight, loved to play BukBuk. If you were Number 3 in the middle or Bufferman, Joe would drop on you determined to break the line. Since I was one of the smallest he often landed on me. We had a pyromaniac who twice set fire to the Mess curtains and we put them out with water and beer. There was a joker who went to sleep in the middle of the road near the WAAF compound. Luckily we were out looking for him at the time.

'Then the war was over and I was detached to Hawarden. When I did go back to clear I was heart-sick. I was told that Joe Pegg had been killed and that "Scouse" Chambers, Phil McGowan, Danny Scopes, Benny Benson, Phil Phillips, Bill Nuttall, Timber Woods and Bob Bloore, all aircrew of one sort or another, had gone on demob. Llanbedr was being killed off and I wanted no part of the Wake. There was the hated long wait for the Barmouth train when I left to join 8 Squadron Tempests in Aden and I did not look back.'

The atomic bomb on Hiroshima on 6th August 1945 drove home to the Allies that military science had been transformed during World War Two. The dreadful potential of nuclear warheads delivered by inter-continental ballistic rockets in any future warfare had to be faced. The British government determined to produce guided weapons and required an overseas rocket range on which to test and develop them, so the possibilities of a joint venture with Canada or Australia were explored.

Len Beadell, 'the last of the true Australian explorers' was asked to delay his Army discharge to conduct the initial surveys for a rocket range at Woomera in South Australia. Later he became Range Reconnaissance Officer at the Weapons Research Establishment and was awarded the British Empire Medal for his work in building the famous Gunbarrel Highway across Central Australia. It was Len Beadell who chose the sites for the first atomic bomb trials at Emu and for the later atomic tests at Maralinga. In 1988 he was awarded the Order of Australia when his achievements were recognised in the Queen's Birthday Honours list.

1946

On a fine morning in March, 631 Squadron pilot, Flying Officer E R Owen, took off from Llanbedr in Spitfire XVI SM472 to practise formation flying. Twenty minutes later he was walking uninjured on the foreshore at Llanfairfechan. However, the incoming tide soon started to engulf the aircraft in which he had made a safe forced landing with wheels and flaps up after experiencing severe engine vibration and a complete loss of engine power.

In England, Tony Whitehead was an RAF Flight Sergeant Air Gunner on Vickers Warwicks when the end of the war led to his retraining as an AC2 Engine Mechanic/Flight Sergeant Air Gunner, one of many aircrew who found themselves in this anomalous situation. Tony was posted to Llanbedr to service the aircraft of 631 Squadron. On arrival he found a 'scruffy ginger-moustached individual sitting in the guardroom skinning a fox, who said that, as there was no one about, I should sleep in the guardroom and meantime visit The Vic for refreshments.' Tony was escorted to The Vic by a 'prisoner awaiting court martial' but 'from my first visit, the welcome to the Victoria Hotel by landlord and customers was so warm that it has remained my favourite hostelry to the present day and I have written fictional stories about it.'

Tony also paid tribute to the famous 'Ma Griff' and her café where she 'fed the Air Force boys at low cost and well beyond the limits of rationing. If any official questioned her she lapsed into a Welsh of her own with no understanding of any other language! I also remember the kind motherly lady who had a café near the bridge. She fed me on many mornings when I missed my breakfast.'

Tony became Sergeants' Mess Caterer with responsibility for the bar and for providing extras paid for by Mess subscriptions. He did not question his 'Good Soldier Svejk' (cheerful Tomas Davis, one of the many German POWs working at Llanbedr) about his mysterious sources for the welcome supplies of chicken, duck, eggs, butter and sugar!

Above: **Tony Whitehead (back row, 3rd from left) with Workshop staff, Llanbedr 1947.**

Right: **Tony Whitehead, an air gunner on Vickers Warwicks, poses by the four-gun tail turret of a Warwick I of 282 Squadron.**

According to Tony, most POWs worked hard and only wished to return home, but there was one SS senior NCO who 'shouted about the virtues of Hitler and National Socialism and tried to stir other prisoners to rebellion, so they decided to transfer him to a de-Nazification unit in East Anglia.' Tony was persuaded to escort him by the offer of a weekend in London en route while the service police looked after the prisoner.

As planned, Tony and his prisoner caught a train that arrived in London too late to allow them to travel on to remote Norfolk before Monday morning. The Paddington military police sent Tony and his prisoner along to the 'London Cage' in Marylebone Road, as Tony recalled: 'There was a high-ranking German Naval officer in his important uniform scrubbing the entrance hall while a large member of the Irish Guards rested a foot on his back. My own prisoner had been a little difficult on the journey, shouting abuse at people on stations and raising my fears that we might become the centre of a riot and end up with

a damaged German. He almost snarled when he spoke to me, obviously holding me in great contempt. But on the Monday morning, when I collected him after my weekend of fun, I found him a changed man! He was quiet with a bowed head and kept calling me either "Sir" or "Flight Sergeant" all the way to Norfolk!'

Australia and Britain agreed to form an equal partnership to create the long-range guided weapons experimental range and village at Woomera and a research & development facility at Salisbury, near Adelaide. Meanwhile a young Australian aeronautical engineer, Ian Fleming, came to Britain for a year's 'attachment' at Royal Aircraft Establishment, Farnborough. Ian's time was divided between two sections – Aero Flight and Aero Projects – which had direct relevance to new project work. This would eventually secure Llanbedr's future target service role for the next half-century and into the 21st century.

In November 1946, Spitfire pilot John Tedder of 631 Squadron was posted to Llanbedr and recalled: 'The squadron also had a few target-towing Martinets, a Harvard for Instrument flying practice and a Tiger Moth for joyriding. The CO, Squadron Leader Joe Pegg was killed in a flying accident and was succeeded by Squadron Leader Richard "Mitch" Mitchell. My Flight Commander was Flight Lieutenant Ken Pugh.'

John remembered the events that followed shortly after one take-off when the engine of his Spitfire started to sputter and the windscreen became covered in oil: 'I was able to complete a circuit and land whereupon my engine stopped. It transpired that the airman who had refuelled my Spitfire had left off the oil filler cap. Much to my disgust he was only given three days CC.' John was also in charge of the Llanbedr Station Library and served as Sports Officer. He was housed in Barmouth and '… it was with great pleasure that I saw my old flat and drinking place – a hotel named CROWN or ROYAL… when I revisited the area in 1994.'

1947

As the Cold War deepened and the first manned supersonic flight was only six months away the 'Anglo-Australian Joint Project' became official. Having returned to Australia, Ian Fleming was offered a new appointment with the Beaufort Division (later titled Government Aircraft Factories) of the Australian Department of Munitions that was undertaking the design and prototype construction of a high-speed pilotless target aircraft to specifications provided by the British Ministry of Supply.

1948

Ian Fleming returned to Britain, with a young draughtsman called Gordon Appelby to discuss the requirement for the high-speed

pilotless target aircraft and to make preliminary design studies. Fleming persuaded the proprietor of their digs to provide them with a table and hunted down a T-square and drawing-paper. He left Gordon at their digs drawing up the schemes while he went out and about to investigate possibilities and gather data, as he recalled: 'The first sight we had of the requirement was a small piece of paper on which were scrawled "500mph at 40,000ft and 75 minutes endurance". The power plant was to be a straight jet development from the Armstrong Siddeley turboprop Mamba engine to give a little more than 1,000lb static thrust at sea level…

'The person from whom I received most encouragement and a great deal of help was George Gardner (Director of Guided Weapons Research & Development), because of his pre-war association with the pilotless Queen Bee development. He ventured that ten flights per aircraft escaping a direct hit, might be a feasible long-term goal. In 1963, when he retired, he was delighted to see his goal being handsomely exceeded!'

Author's Note: In 1989 Australian target controller Ben Dannecker wrote: 'Here's a friendly gauntlet for you. Our local record for the number of flights completed by one Jindivik is still the 324 flights made by N11-530 before it was ditched in the Tasman Sea in 1987 following irrecoverable autopilot problems.' At that time Engineering Manager George Hobbs said that Llanbedr's highest number of sorties flown by one Jindi was 133, with another Jindi at 129 and several just past their centuries. 'But ours are fired at more often!' George pointed out. Subsequently a Llanbedr Jindivik reached 265 flights before being destroyed after missile damage. Today there is no contest as Jindivik flying in Australia has ended.

Within three months of returning to Australia, Ian's group received the go-ahead to design both piloted and pilotless variants and to build two piloted and six pilotless prototypes. Ian was reluctant to spend time on the manned version because 'there was little enough space for the fuel and equipment needed for pilotless operation, let alone a pilot, his cockpit controls and instruments and an acceptable undercarriage system.' However the result in time and cost would have been about the same by either route, Ian Fleming conceded afterwards.

While Pika (Project A) and Jindivik (Project B) took shape on Australian drawing-boards, on the other side of the world, 631 Squadron was maintaining a target service at Llanbedr with six Spitfires, three Martinets and a Harvard.

After a radio course at Yatesbury, Bill Williamson was posted to the Signals Section at RAF Llanbedr. 'It seemed like a foreign country,' remembered Bill. 'When the train stopped at Barmouth there was Welsh being spoken all around me. But the people were friendly, the scenery picturesque and there were balmy breezes and sunshine. I will never forget Llanbedr for the great time, the comrades there and the dances. It was paradise!' Firstly, Bill met Corporal 'Paddy' Mulloy, '... lolling over the handrail as I approached the guardroom, his ginger hair shining under his white-topped hat, looking for trouble as was his wont.' Bill also remem-

bered the CO, Squadron Leader Hindlay, as a well-liked, nice and understanding person.

In Bill's section there was Battersby (' "Ma Griff's" best customer'), Lionel Trusker and Corporal Jeff Taylor. The aircrew included P1 Jock Hutchinson who flew English Electric Lightnings when they first arrived; Flight Lieutenant 'Pug-H' Pugh, the Flight Commander; and P2 Cowling, who played the piano and was killed in a flying accident. Bill also recalled Station Warrant Officer Templeton who was soon to become a postman but first had to learn to ride a bicycle: 'I saw two airmen holding the large SWO upright on a bike teaching him to ride it! One of the best was Warrant Officer McFadyen, who had been taken prisoner in Crete, but returned to the RAF after the war.'

Bill recalled the death of Leading Aircraftman Colin Cell, who volunteered for 'one of the most dirty, dangerous and unpleasant duties – target-towing' and was drowned on his first trip. When the pilot throttled back to deposit the drogue and then opened up again, there was no response and the Martinet sank into the sea. The lifeboat found the pilot, P1 Davis, sitting in a dinghy, but the airman was face down in the water. P2 Cowling, who was popular for playing the NAAFI

631 Squadron at Llanbedr.

piano to entertain the 'erks', was also killed when his rudder was damaged by P1 Davis' aircraft manoeuvring too close. Cowling crashed into the sea off Holyhead while Davis managed to recover his own aircraft to Llanbedr.

Corporal Mulloy appears to have received his comeuppance after a Saturday night in Barmouth. He sat next to the driver of a gharry carrying 20 airmen and airwomen who went dancing or to the cinema. They returned at 0100hrs and Corporal Mulloy changed into full uniform and then charged all the occupants of the gharry with being later than 2359hrs back to camp. By common consent he was promptly thrown into the emergency water tank!

1949

Early in the year 631 Squadron was renumbered 20 Squadron, and operated Beaufighters, Spitfires and Vampires until July when Llanbedr ceased to be a fighter station. In the following month the squadron moved with its Beaufighters and Vampires to RAF Valley, the Vampires being the first jet-propelled aircraft to be based there. This was the year when a General Duties clerk asked Jack Forster if he wanted to be a pilot for his national service and Jack thought 'it seemed like a good idea'. RAFVR pilot Don Reed made a flying visit to Llanbedr in an Anson, to collect some meat for a luncheon to be held at his Castle Bromwich Officers' Mess. It was supplied by RAFVR Wing Commander Angus McLean, of the Lion Hotel, Criccieth and was 'a bit stringy', but this didn't prevent Don from returning to Llanbedr a few years later to share a crew-room with Jack Forster.

The Ministry of Supply wished to update the E.7/48 specification to provide for a faster target and Ian Fleming was asked to do a design study using a reheated Adder engine, developed from the earlier Mamba engine. Mach 9.0 to 9.5 over a height range from 30,000-50,000 feet, was acceptable, but then the more stringent Specification No. U22/49 was issued seeking a target more realistically representative of an enemy aircraft. However Ian Fleming's work was not yet ready to secure the future of Llanbedr airfield so the station was run down until only a Care and Maintenance party was left. National serviceman Desmond O'Reilly of Brentwood, Essex, remembered: 'My days at Llanbedr were very happy ones. I was one of the 14 people who completed the work of closing down this Fighter Command station. It was great to learn that it became operational again and was still going at the end of the century.'

Below left: **Bill Williamson (2nd from right) with colleagues, 1949.**

Below right: **'Care & Maintenance' outside the telephone exchange, 1949.**

Chapter Three

The 1950s

No windsock flew at Llanbedr for several months while the British Army trained there for the Korean War. When aerial targets were needed, 20 (AAC) Squadron flew their Beaufighter TT.10s, Spitfire LF.XVIEs and Vampire F.1s from RAF Valley. The squadron subsequently became No.5 Civilian Anti-Aircraft Co-operation Unit (CAACU) in 1951 and acquired Mosquito and Meteor target tugs but, on returning to Llanbedr, came under the control of RAF Maintenance Command. However, because the civilian contractor, Short Brothers & Harland Ltd, employed ex-service pilots and engineers the RAF supervisors were eventually phased out. The unit served the Army artillery ranges at Tonfannau and Ty Croes.

In October 1950 the UK's guided missile programme received the same priority as an all-British atomic bomb, increasing the need for a pilotless target aircraft against which air-to-air and surface-to-air missiles could be tested. Jindivik development was running late, so RAE Farnborough began experimenting with 'droning' Fairey Firefly aircraft.

In Australia the first of two Pikas was loaded aboard a Bristol Freighter at Fisherman's Bend and delivered to Woomera. On 31 October GAF test pilot John Miles planned to get the Pika airborne for 100 yards or so and to put it down again. But the Pika (a 'tail-dragger') declined to raise its tail. After some calculations on the back of an envelope Ian Fleming suggested that John should try 20° flap for take-off. The aircraft promptly leaped almost 100 feet into the air before John could put it down again! The next flight satisfied everyone but on the third the undercarriage would not come down. A skilful belly landing ensured that two weeks later the aircraft was repaired and flying again.

The Pika manned proof-of-concent aircraft flying at Woomera, South Australia.

1951

More test pilots were brought in and the two Pikas made 214 flights between October 1950 and June 1954. As Ian Fleming noted: 'They were used not only for proving the basic design concepts and the automatic control system, but also for Jindivik crew training.' Pika demonstrated that a rudder wasn't necessary on Jindivik, thus making great savings in weight, time and money.

Wing Commander Fred Knudsen of Tugun, Queensland remembered operating Pika: 'On the take-off roll you didn't get any decent rudder or elevator control until about 80 knots, so crosswind take-offs weren't on. Forward visibility was poor until you raised the tail. The controls were extra-sensitive and the actual take-off was like walking on eggs. The aircraft flew nicely, climbing at about 350 knots. I believe I did the only high Mach number flying, reaching about 0.95 without any problems.'

Armstrong Siddeley produced a higher-thrust engine and Ian Fleming began work on a Jindivik Mk 2. Before the Jindivik Mk 1 made its maiden flight, GAF received another order, for six more Mk 1 prototypes with the Adder engine AND four Mk 2 prototypes with the Viper turbojet.

At Llanbedr, teenage 'Katie' became Technical Secretary to Short's chief engineer. She married a colleague and became Mrs George Brown. Apart from a motherhood break, Katie worked at the airfield until 1991 along with Deputy Chief Radio Engineer N Collins, Airframe Supervisor L 'Jimmy' Dobson, Charlie R Harris (Chief Storekeeper), Ralph Highley (Deputy Chief Jindivik Engineer), W A Howie (Mechanical Transport Officer), W J Jones (Deputy Chief Aircraft Engineer), T D Newett (Engine Supervisor), G Owen (Engine Supervisor), E E Phillips (Electrical Supervisor), Dennis Rossell (Chief Aircraft Engineer), T G Trenholme (Electrical Supervisor), G I Williams (Jindivik Airframe Supervisor) and Miss J G Jones who, as Dennis Rossell noted, was famous for 'providing clean offices and good cuppas!'

In a beautiful Welsh autumn, 20 Squadron was disbanded and Dennis 'Ross' Rossell, an ex-Halton apprentice who had been a crew chief at West Malling during the early days of World War Two, arrived to make his mark at Llanbedr for the next 23 years before his early death.

1952

In Australia, Jindivik development flying was having more downs than ups! The first two attempts at take-off with the Jindivik Mk 1 prototype, from its launch trolley, were failures. Someone omitted to uncage the directional gyroscope on the trolley so it was fuelled off because it was not running straight. On the next attempt the electrical failure of a micro-switch spoiled the unstick sequence and the aircraft went off the end of the runway into the rough. However on 28th August the combination of launch trolley with Jindivik perched on top ran true; the light flashed up the start of the 'unstick' sequence and the Jindivik flew cleanly off the trolley and climbed away. At this stage the 'Anglo-Saxon' remarks of the Skipper, Flight Lieutenant Tom Berry and the Navigator, Flight Sergeant 'Blue' Gallagher were put down to the pleasure of the achievement. The satisfaction and excitement lasted half an hour while remote control of the Jindivik was alternated between the crew on the ground and an airborne controller, with a control transmitter, in a dual-seat Meteor shepherd aircraft.

When the time came to make an approach the signal 'land glide' was sent, to lower the flaps and landing skid and to reduce the rpm. Immediately the Jindivik pitched up and stalled. The nose dropped and the aircraft regained flying speed until it pitched up and stalled again, and again, and again! The airborne controller in the shepherding Meteor tried to land it safely away from the airfield but the Jindivik was written off. An excessive elevator trim setting in the automatic pilot was adjusted and development flying continued but by the end of the year three Mk 1 prototypes had been lost in 15 sorties while other Jindiviks and Pikas suffered repairable damage.

Controlling the aircraft was not easy, as Fred Knudsen recalled: 'In the back of the

Mk 7 Meteor I had a set of Jindivik controls with which I often flew the Jindivik by remote control while we flew in formation with it. There were anxious moments when the Jindivik started to turn INSIDE our Meteor. On two occasions when the Jindivik engine flamed out I tried to force-land the aircraft in one of the dry lake-beds of the Woomera area. I had one failure and one moderate success!'

In the UK, to fill the gap until Jindivik was ready, the Fairey Firefly T.7 was selected for modification to become a pilotless target drone (designated the U.8) after flight trials were carried out by Flight Lieutenants Peter Pennie and J S Knight. The Royal Navy no longer required Fireflies, and trials began using the in-line three-seat aircraft with the 'black boxes' fitted into the centre-seat position. Llanbedr was chosen as the operating base and a team from Farnborough familiarised the Short Brothers & Harland pilots and ground crews with the aircraft handling and servicing. No.5 CAACU was already operating at Llanbedr in conjunction with contractors Short Brothers & Harland Ltd so servicing of the Firefly's airframe and Rolls-Royce Griffon 59 engine, plus the provision of airfield services and of safety pilots were also eventually subcontracted to Short Brothers & Harland Ltd.

The 'black boxes' were the province of 'Wilkie' Wilkinson, Ralph Sage and Tommy Harle of Farnborough's Instrument and Photographic (IAP) Section until a special RAF unit was formed by Flight Lieutenant Sean Scanlon to look after them and provide ground control, radar crews and rear-seat observers for the Fireflies. While IAP was modifying a standard Mk 9 autopilot the Radio department (which included Geoff Taylor, an Australian engineer) developed air and ground radio control systems. Other RAF test pilots were Flight Lieutenant (later promoted to Squadron Leader) Ken Ashley and Flight Lieutenant 'Foggy' Knight.

Sean Scanlon eventually gathered Flight Sergeant Roddie Veitch, Sergeants Derek Whitehead, Reg Smith and Hartley Shallcross at Llanbedr airfield. 'A jolly good selection it turned out to be,' remembered Sean. 'Sergeant Derek Whitehead was the first. He moved up from Aberporth with an auto-follow radar to be used for setting the drone on track outbound and for positioning it in the circuit on return.'

At Farnborough it was found that a great deal of flying time was needed on the Firefly, but the airfield was very busy so the Firefly development team made one-day detachments to other airfields. The RAE was committed to the task of destroying a target aircraft in flight with a guided missile by early 1954, this being known as 'Trial Q'. The missile was to be a beam-riding rocket test vehicle – RTV1(e). However, this project was no further advanced than the pilotless Firefly programme!

A catapult launch system was also being developed because the Ministry of Supply and the RAE thought that a manual take-off by remote control would be unacceptably dangerous. An expensive pre-stressed concrete base was laid at Llanbedr near the edge of Runway 24. For propulsion it was intended to use 16 5-inch rockets for each take-off. This system was discarded when Sean managed to convince the top brass that his team could just '… drive the thing off the runway by simple coarse rudder control.' Sean admitted afterwards that: '… on one occasion some pilots and a chap painting a hangar roof at Farnborough were a bit frightened during this process! Take-off control was a personal knack not necessarily possessed by pilots, even test pilots!'

At Farnborough, while serving in the RAF, Reg Smith helped to assemble the remote control electronics. Transmitters were fitted into a 3-ton Bedford pantechnicon while the airborne equipment went into the Firefly U.8 and was coupled to the autopilot, throttle, flaps and undercarriage systems. Reg Smith recalled those early days with the new drone: 'We practised radio-controlled take-offs and landings, much to the alarm of the regular denizens of Farnborough and other long-suffering airfields like Chilbolton and Dunsfold. During this period we had a real live pilot on board, from the Empire Test Pilots School, to take over when things got a bit too hairy.'

In November 1951 the first Firefly AS.7 arrived at Llanbedr in the shape of WJ147, dubbed 'Cuckoo in the Nest'. It was the fore-runner of the Firefly U.8 target aircraft, to come from the Firefly AS.7 and the T.7 observer/radar operator trainer version of the AS.7; and also of the later Firefly U.9 target aircraft, converted from the Firefly Mk 4 and Mk 5. Around this time a young fitter called Alun Jones started his career at Llanbedr and on retirement at the end of the 20th century he held the record for the longest continuous service (45 years) at Llanbedr airfield. As Alun noted, his record will last '...probably thereafter unless young Kevin Hobbs stays here until he retires, when he might beat my record, just!'

1953

Reg Smith recalled how he and his colleagues were 'banished to the wilds of North Wales where, if we did anything wrong, the resultant debris could be expected to fall in the sea rather than on someone's head.' They installed ground control equipment in Building 29, laid land-lines around Llanbedr airfield to the ends of each of the runways and practised drone operations using the mobile installation transported to Llanbedr from Farnborough.

'By the time I joined RAE Llanbedr there were only refinements to be carried out before the great day when our experimental aircraft made its first hands-off landing, with the test pilot in the cockpit, his hands firmly positioned behind his head and shouting: "EUREKA!" ' said Rod 'Chiefy' Veitch.

Derek Whitehead and his fellow RAF technicians brought with them their American Type SCR 584 search/lock-on radar set: 'This radar was originally sent over to Britain for tracking and locking on to German V1 and V2 bombs/rockets at which it was considerably successful,' recalled Derek. 'It was regarded as portable and had the capability of locking on to a target in azimuth and elevation, but range had to be tracked manually. It was hauled up onto a flattened sand-hill over-looking Llanbedr airfield and a Dobbie McCinnis plotting table was hastily acquired which was installed in the top of a corrugated-metal control tower, designed by RAE Aberporth and built nearby.

'The system worked well and with the help of a remote optical antenna positioner the radar was locked on to the drone target virtually on take-off. Later on, to improve lock-on and to save time at greater distances, an Army MZPI search radar was also hauled up onto a sand-hill.'

In May 1953, Short's pilot Don Reed arrived with Ted Primey to fly for the Naval Ferry Flight, based at Llanbedr. They took turns to fly the Royal Navy de Havilland Dominie and drop the other pilot at specified airfields for ferrying Fireflies, Supermarine Seafires, Percival Sea Princes and North American Harvards. At weekends they were often sent to Belfast to fly Airspeed Oxfords on Fighter Control interceptions or to RAF Woodvale to fly for the Reserve Flying School.

Jindivik development flying continued in Australia. Four Jindiviks were lost during 26 sorties, one of which was a Mk 2 prototype with a short-life engine. What Ian Fleming later described as its 'simple and cheap' fuel system (The Sir Lawrence Wackett Lecture, 1977) wouldn't accept any power setting below maximum! When all attempts to stop this Jindivik from tearing around at top speed failed, the aircraft was 'fuelled off' and crashed away from base. Thereafter Jindivik Mk 2s were fitted with Bristol Siddeley Viper turbojets with normal fuel control systems and pumps.

According to Ian Fleming, although the Jindivik Mk 2 had almost the same planform and configuration as the Mk 1, in the detail it was a completely new design that took advantage of the extra thrust to improve the Mach number from 0.73 to 0.85 and to increase the Jindivik's operational ceiling to over 48,000 feet.

This was the year of Jindivik Mk 1 trials at Woomera. Rob Nash related how, on it's second flight, Jindivik A92-11 failed to separate from the launch trolley and took it along for the ride! Under the control of the shepherd an emergency landing of this unusual combination was attempted gingerly on Lake Hart, a dry salt-lake bed. The soft surface caused the wheels to bog down, but afterwards both aircraft and trolley were repairable and A92-11 went on to make three more flights.

Rob also reported that on some of the early hair-raising trials the Jindivik seemed to develop a mind of its own, stubbornly ignoring its master's commands, making suicidal low-level passes over the desert or sudden aggressive darts at the shepherd aircraft. On another occasion when the Shepherd lost sight of the Jindivik the radar transponder also failed. For 30 minutes the position of the Jindivik was 'not known'. Then, miraculously, the Shepherd spotted it. After being in the air for over an hour the Jindivik was landed without incident.

In 1953 Alan Hawkins arrived at Llanbedr 'and was the passenger in Firefly WJ153 which, following engine failure, did a fairly comprehensive self-destruct during a forced landing [on 22nd April] at Rhosmaeloan Farm, Dinas Dinlle. I was told later that "any landing you walk away from is a good one". Dicky Dickenson, the pilot, limped away with a twisted ankle while I had a cut finger. I was told: "Tomorrow laddie, you're up in a Mosquito – they've got two engines!"'

Reg Smith heard the pilot's Mayday call when the Firefly's engine stopped and listened anxiously. He heard: 'It's OK, I've got the booster pump running and it's picked up again. I'll try and make base…' followed by: 'It's no use, the f****** thing has stopped altogether now!' Reg recalled subsequent events: 'We waited until we heard they were both OK and then mounted an expedition to recover the wing-tip camera pods which were still on the Secret list!'

The *Daily Post* told the story on 23rd April, reporting: 'RAF plane crashes in field near Llandwrog' and stating that the field was owned by Mr William M Griffith who had run to the scene with Gordon Roberts and Richard Parry. Mrs Ann Griffith had taken tea to Alan and his pilot who suffered minor injuries and shock.

Geoff Taylor's diary for July reads: 'Set off for Llanbedr in the 3-ton Radio van and the Hillman utility with Sergeant Reg Smith and my wife Lorna (an illegal passenger) … Lovely scenery along Lake Bala. The 3-tonner a bit wide for the narrow roads! … Ensconced in old Cae Nest farmhouse … We all (Lorna and CO's wife included) cleaned out the old huts and installed the ground

The metal control tower designed and built by Aberporth.

The original SCR 584 with Optical Tracker on the flattened sand-hill.

equipment while Derek Whitehead's group set up the radar and other facilities. We got unexplained cable faults due to the local hare colony so Tom Harle's shotgun provided some tasty meals at Cae Nest! But Oh! How it rained that summer! We put our wetness into verse to a well-known Welsh tune:

Land of our exile so peaceful and green
The soggiest country that ever was seen
The rain piddles down in an unceasing stream
You'll need all your wellies in Wales

'The chorus was worse, beginning:
Wales, Wales, the pubs shut on Sundays in Wales ...'

The Firefly Control Centre caravan was perched on a sand-hill. Sean Scanlon sat in front of a sloping metal panel with push-buttons for each command, and a heading indicator which, when aligned with the drone heading, followed one-degree port or starboard change-of-course commands. Prominent was the 'Emergency Ditch' button, with a cylindrical enclosure and lid. The word 'Elsan' was written on the original version, Alan Hawkins claimed. A command analogue two-tones-from-eight system was used and as there was no telemetry for the ground crews to monitor the behaviour of the drone, they relied on continuous observation by the Firefly 'Shepherd' aircraft.

Alan was sitting in the rear cockpit of a Firefly on a trial rehearsal when they had a height-lock freeze-up and suddenly went into a steepish dive. It was policy to wait and do nothing to give the drone control system a chance to correct itself. But on this occasion it didn't and eventually safety pilot Dicky Dickenson transmitted: 'Target aircraft now in 60-degree dive – have lost it!' Honour was satisfied and Dicky could hit the cut-out button and pull out of the dive 'before we upset the population of Aberystwyth!' explained Alan.

1954

The crunch came in January, noted Geoff Taylor, the Australian Experimental Officer, who was tasked with adapting the Jindivik radio control gear to suit the Firefly and setting up the first radio control installation at Llanbedr: 'Time to prove to the Americans that a Brit missile could down a Brit target! In spite of having a slight landing problem we were to get the damn thing airborne and down the range to Aberporth whether or not we could get it back, and it was all to be very secret.'

Below: **The Aberporth detachment at Llanbedr.**

Photographs on the opposite page:

The first pilotless Firefly being readied for take-off at Llanbedr on 3rd February 1954.

An early Fairey Firefly UAV in flight.

After the first flight of a pilotless Firefly.

'We were not allowed a pilotless test flight with our Firefly although there had been plenty of test firings of the RTV missile,' reported Sean Scanlon. 'But we had practised with a safety pilot on board and with overall direction by the Aberporth air controller. We had worked out the "racetrack" pattern and timings to steer the target into a defined small "box" when it would be hit by the RTV. More of a controlled collision of the target with the missile than an interception of the target by the RTV!'

Sean ruled that each pilotless aircraft was to be accompanied by an Observer Shepherd aircraft (to report by radio) and that the Shepherd crew would check out the drone target aircraft before launching. But on 3rd February, with snow on the surrounding mountains, Firefly U.8 WJ150 was taxied out and positioned on the threshold of Runway 23. The pilot and accompanying technician completed their checks, climbed out and closed the canopy, leaving the drone with the engine running and the tailwheel resting behind a small chock, awaiting the Master Controller's remote command to 'Take Off and Climb'.

'Squadron Leader Ken Ashley had flown in from Farnborough to observe the flight from the air using his own aircraft,' recalled Sean. 'But, after he'd watched the launch of the pilotless target his own aircraft failed to start so he pinched the Firefly that was waiting for Dickie Dickenson, the Shepherd pilot.'

Alan Hawkins described how the tenseness of this first Q (unmanned) Trial was broken shortly after take-off, by the voices of Ralph Sage and Wilky singing: 'Ken Ashley now our Shepherd is; He flies the famous Firefly. His job is just to take a quiz; Sean Scanlon's work to simplify.'

There were heart-stopping moments when Alan's team appeared to lose the reset pulses for the emergency shutdown timer that would, if not reset, 'time out' in 90 seconds and short out the magnetos. Full down elevator would be applied to destroy the aircraft by diving it into the sea! However, the system was reset in time.

The Take-Off Controller at the end of Runway 24 required skill and luck to prevent the torque of the Griffon engine taking the plane off the right-hand side of the runway – and the second attempt to provide an unmanned target ended in just this manner. Another difficulty was that the retract signal for the landing gear was usually given as it reached full extension. However, the aircraft tended to lift off in a series of hops so, there was the risk of the drone touching down again during or after retraction of the landing gear. So they set the control column back a certain distance based on the assumption that because the autopilot had a slow reaction time at slow speeds, this amount of 'up-elevator' would keep the aircraft on the runway longer and thus lead to a cleaner lift-off!

For landing, the Azimuth Controller was on the peritrack and in line with the centre of Runway 16, holding a Left/Right control and looking through powerful tripod-mounted binoculars. His briefing was straightforward: 'Acquire the target, get it on the graticule and, when you can see only the prop and spinner, grab the binoculars and run!' A periscope positioned at the south end of Runway 16 and designed to see over a 'hump' in the runway, was in fact little used as the Azimuth Controller could put the target on the runway centreline successfully without it, explained Alan.

The Pitch Controller, to the west of the runway, had a gyro gunsight. With the graticule on the target, signals were fed to a mechanical computer which sent up/down-elevator signals to maintain the correct approach angle and then a series of up-elevator signals to attain the landing attitude and reduce the rpm to idle. The Firefly had a tendency to bounce and then the trailing hook failed to engage a wire. This was a great relief to Sergeant Vic Kemp's arrester gear party because a successful landing engagement required two hours of hard work to get the roller chain, wires and discs collected and rerigged.

Reg Smith also described their first pilotless Firefly sortie: 'With some trepidation we sent it off. They fired their round, and missed, so we were faced with getting the thing back. We had three attempts to land it, ending with a ground loop. Still it was in one piece and ready next day. We weren't – having had a monumental thrash the night before.'

Top: **Dickie Dickenson and Brian Axworthy exit the cockpits after a Firefly sortie.**

Above: **Alan Grummitt and Derek Barton in Firefly WB352 abeam the Dyffryn Seaside Estate.**

Right: **Reg Smith and Brian Axworthy with a pilotless Firefly after its undercarriage failed to lower for landing.**

Top left: **Reg Smith with radio control gear.**

Top right: **Jimmy Barratt on 'Pitch control'.**

There were more unmanned flights and frequent practising for the team to gain confidence by the time the Firestreak air-to-air missile arrived. 'We had supplied targets for several missiles by then, but Firestreak was special!' recalled Reg. For this 'high priority' trial the team worked 11-hour days, seven days a week for five weeks, after which they had one Sunday afternoon off! Another two weeks without a break followed and the trial was completed. During this period they prepared two or three aircraft every day and actually supplied 11 unmanned targets. For the first ten sorties the firing was cancelled AFTER the target was airborne, mostly because the missile batteries were flat.

The eleventh pilotless sortie was different, Reg recalled: 'On the r/t we heard the fighter pilot (Callsign "Murex 3", usually misread as "Durex 3"!) describe the flight of the missile towards the target and then a triumphant yell of "Got it!" Aberporth and Valley were over the moon and Llanbedr's feeling of loss was alleviated by the hope we might have a normal five-day week now they had got rid of that missile!'

More pilotless flights followed, with Firestreak scoring the highest percentage of direct hits. The team became skilled at bringing back target aircraft that were damaged or had suffered partial systems failures in the air due to hits. Nevertheless, some aircraft were lost due to take-off or landing accidents.

'Sean Scanlon once brought back an aircraft from 30 miles away using the joystick in the control tower in response to r/t instructions from the shepherd pilot,' stated Reg. 'The target kept climbing or diving due to a faulty potentiometer in the autopilot. By the time Sean handed it to the landing sights we were in a sweat, but it actually behaved quite well on the approach and of course we could now see it. Once, a target wouldn't turn left so we approached at an angle, timing the blips of right turn so that the last corrections were applied as the aircraft crossed the runway threshold. We were a small unit with a very high workload but morale was terrific, due largely to Sean Scanlon. The success of the Firefly drone and Firestreak owe much to this.

'I operated Coarse Azimuth until mid-1956. I stood at the north end of Runway 16, steered the Firefly down the centreline, over my head and into the arrester gear and beyond if we missed the wires! All I had was tripod-mounted binoculars, and a joystick marked "Left-Right". Jim Barratt operated the Pitch Sight under a significant disadvantage using an "automatic" sight. He had to compensate for its shortcomings and became very good at controlling the descent. I trusted him to fly aircraft low over my head several times a day!

'We did miss the wires fairly frequently, but we developed our own techniques. If we had no wind (rare), a tailwind or a crosswind from port we would agree between us that we must definitely take the wires. But with a reasonable headwind, say ten knots, and a small starboard crosswind component, we could safely afford to miss the wires. At the crucial moment the Firefly would sail past, a few inches too high. I would then steer it off the runway to starboard and up the slope of the airfield to come to rest on the grass about halfway between the intersection and the end of Runway 24.'

Chief Aircraft Engineer Dennis Rossell declared that the early days of Firefly operations were: 'Interesting and downright frightening. Landing was an extremely hazardous operation; the aircraft had to approach so that its arrester hook would engage one of the five wires laid across the runway to which tons of heavy anchor chains were attached. Sod's Law or Murphy's Law often caused the Firefly to bounce over the wires and develop a swing before being caught by the "Christ Almighty!" wire some hundreds of yards further on. The sudden attachment to this wire caused the aircraft to drift violently and often its undercarriage collapsed. The Firefly was then "crash-recovered" and categorised. If it was salvageable it went to "Dr Jack Cleaver and his Merry Men" of Fairey's working party who did major repairs on site. But "heavy landing" checks, propeller shaft shock-load tests, prop changes, engine changes and wing changes were accepted as routine maintenance actions.

Early Firefly ops at Llanbedr.

'My deputy Bill Jones was highly proficient in "Prang Recovery". He could clear the runway of a "three-point landing mishap" as follows: If the propeller hubs and mainwheels were touching the ground it took him nine minutes. If it was a "Full Belly Flop" then 20 minutes were needed. But if the aircraft was "in the mud" then it was a three-day job!'

Ross was less tolerant over the maintenance of the Royal Navy Dominie aircraft and wrote it off for corrosion. Fortunately the ferry pilots Don Reed and Ted Primey were fed up and asked if they could join No.5 CAACU permanently. The Airfield Manager was about to invite them to do so and all parties were content. Don described the Llanbedr operation at that time:

'The main buildings were Air Traffic Control and the hangar and there were two short runways. The Manager's office was on the ground floor of Air Traffic along with the Secretary's office and Sick Quarters. Upstairs was the Air Traffic room with the desk in the centre, the locker room and pilot's crew room on the left. The telephone exchange was just inside the door and the RAF detachment occupied the right-hand end while they waited for their first building (29) to be available.

'CAACU served Tonfannau, just north of Towyn and Ty Croes in Anglesey and the two

main exercises were Z6 (at 6,000 feet) for the heavy guns and X1.5 (1,500 feet) for the light ones. The runs could be for live firing at a towed sleeve or silent (no firing), in a dumb-bell pattern with 360° turns at each end along the front of the guns. Firstly Beaufighters were used and then the Mosquito TT.35 and the towed sleeves would be "ordinary" or "radar" type, the sleeve having a wire mesh. For silent runs mainly Spitfire LF.XVIs or Vampire F.3s or FB.5s were used. Sometimes we had to pass in front of the guns in a gentle curve or, approaching from the sea, run straight at the guns. Our winch operators were Edwyn Lewis, "Hoppy" Hopkins and "Red" Redford. On one occasion Norman Sharp was flying the Z6 pattern and live shells were bursting above, below and on both sides of his aircraft. The Range Manager was most apologetic and laid on a big party afterwards for all the pilots!'

Eric Ralphs of Stoke-on-Trent saw these operations from the gunners' point of view: 'I was trained at Tonfannau in the art of shooting down aircraft! The drogues came from Llanbedr via a Beaufighter and our 3.7-inch guns blazed away at huge expense one glorious summer. The light AA guns (Bofors 20mm) were also in constant action. The most accurate TA Camp Battery came from Stoke-on-Trent and I remember they removed the drogue every time!'

Jindivik development was still slow and the need for a high-speed/high-altitude target was increasing, so the drone conversion programme continued with Meteor F.4s and F.8s as they were available from the RAF. Flight Refuelling Ltd at Tarrant Rushton in Dorset was tasked with the conversion work and at RAE Farnborough Peter Pennie was the test pilot for preliminary trials in Meteor T.7 VW413.

At Woomera, when the last Jindivik Mk 1 flight was made in October, only one of the 12 Mk 1s remained serviceable. The loss rate was very disappointing but eventually one was used as a guided weapons target and the years of painstaking development work were rewarded. One problem was the tendency of the aircraft to bounce after touching down. This difficulty was resolved by fitting a 'sting' that extended below the skid when the Jindivik was in the landing configuration. On contacting the ground the 'sting' operated a switch that cut off the fuel and retracted the landing flaps. This took out the bounce!

In the UK, youthful pilot Jack Forster enjoyed a cigarette and relaxed in the right-hand seat of an Anson trundling from Alder-grove to Bovingdon. Then he made his acquaintanceship (the first of many) with drone operations at Llanbedr when he noticed a red and yellow Firefly with empty cockpits flying alongside. With horror they realised they were in drone target airspace in Cardigan Bay! Diving away, they scuttled across the sea to sneak inland around Newquay. Jack went on to renew his acquaintanceship (legitimately) with Llanbedr's red and yellow pilotless aircraft several times in later decades. Also during 1954, Ray Tyson joined the technical staff to begin his long-term career at Llanbedr.

Before the end of the year a Meteor U.15 (EE524) arrived at Melbourne Docks en route for Woomera. Originally built for the RAF by Armstrong Whitworth, this aircraft began life as an F.4 and was the first to be converted to a U.15 drone by Flight Refuelling Ltd, the RAF having re-equipped with the Meteor F.8. Flight Lieutenant H J Dodgson, later to serve at Llanbedr, piloted the drone to RAAF Edinburgh Field in South Australia.

1955

At RAE Farnborough the first Meteor take-off under automatic control was successfully carried out on 17th January with Peter Pennie as safety pilot, and an observer and on 11th March they attempted the first pilotless fully automatic landing under ground control. Unfortunately the attempt resulted in a heavy landing that drove the undercarriage through the aircraft's wings. After that incident a safety pilot was carried on all development test flights.

Back at Llanbedr another memorable personality arrived – airframe fitter Charlie Meadows – to work on the line with Alun Jones. The aircraft line-up at the time included Mosquitoes, Vampires, Beaufighters, Oxfords, Fireflies and a Meteor. Forty-

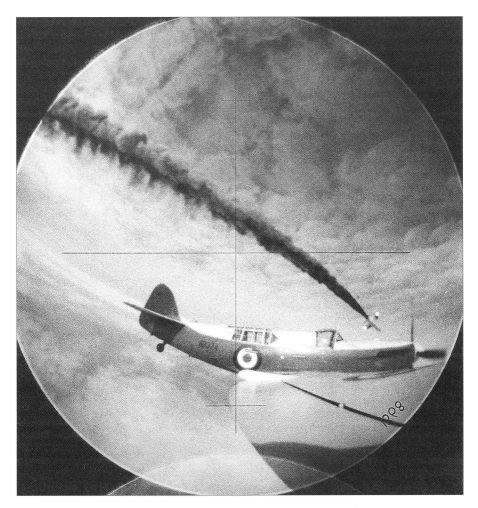

A wing-tip camera on Firefly U.9 WB374 records the passage of a missile.

five years later, there was *still* a Meteor at Llanbedr, thanks to Charlie's struggles to find the parts, ways and means to keep it flying.

In the early 1950s, remembered Charlie, the airfield boasted no title, it was just 'Llanbedr'. There was no gate guard and no gate! 'Summer holiday traffic, enjoying their right of way to Shell Island, was confronted by the sight of aircraft, propellers spinning, coming at them head on. The effect was lines of shunted cars and jack-knifed caravans. Fortunately, the pilot's suggestions, shouted through the clear vision panel, as to what the holiday-maker should do with his caravan, were drowned out by the roar of Merlin engines!

'Day after day our Mosquito and Beaufighter aircraft flew the short distance to Tonfannau, returning to drop the tattered remains of a drogue and then to stream out another. The job was not without its dangers as the zeal of the gunners often exceeded their accuracy. Shells would burst in front of the towing aircraft or sever the towing cable only yards behind it, which caused interesting banter on the r/t. Pilots would cast aspersions on the gunners' parentage or assist them with instructions such as "the target is on the other end of the f*****g wire".'

Life was tough for winch operators, particularly in the Beaufighter, where they shared the rear fuselage with the winch drum and mechanism and a supply of target sleeves. They had to tie the target lanyard to the winch cable before dispatching it through a chute in the floor. The winch drum and brake would become hot and give off clouds of smoke so the winch operator would emerge from the aircraft with black rings around his eyes and tears streaming down his face. 'There was a high turnover of winch operators who, having been once lured into the air, would rapidly decide to give up the opulent lifestyle afforded by the extra two shillings and sixpence per week flight pay!' said Charlie.

Flight Lieutenant 'Jimmy' W C James, an RAF engineer from the RAE Guided Weapons Department, joined the Firefly team in 1955. He recalled flying the converted Navy aircraft: 'Take-offs were not too bad but no matter what the pitch controller did, the output from the aircraft's autopilot pitch control loop could not result in the elevators being moved quickly enough to provide accurate last-minute (second) corrections for landing. Also there was no ready way of providing a short burst of engine power as a pilot might do (and Dicky Dickenson often did!) to help ease aircraft onto the ground after a bounce.'

Charlie Meadows wondered why the Ground Tracking Radar facility was always switched off just as the drone went out of sight. As a consequence, a large section of the workforce had to be out on the airfield 'listening' to establish the whereabouts of the returning aircraft! Reg Smith explained that when an Army team was readying a SAM for launching from Aberporth, the round went off prematurely. It was thought that the nearby search radar had injected just enough energy into the igniter circuits to fire the missile's motor. The soldier was holding up the plug and socket connection to the motor igniters so that the Launcher Safety Officer could see that all was safe, and this probably acted as an antenna. 'Thereafter, as a precaution (and perhaps to share the blame),

we at Llanbedr, 40 miles away, also had to switch off our radar whenever a launch was imminent. This certainly made Derek Whitehead's job far more difficult,' said Reg.

Derek Whitehead and his colleagues attended further training by Standard Telephone and Cables at Southgate, north London, and returned to Llanbedr with 'a shiny new (the very latest)' Precision Approach Radar. The console was installed on the first floor of the metal tower and provided what Derek described as 'more accurate tracking and control on the approach in poor visibility'. His team was responsible for operating and maintaining the equipment.

Serving with the RAF detachment was Instrument Technician Brian Axworthy who also flew as an Observer in Fireflies and later in Meteors. Past experience of the Smith's Mk 9 autopilot brought Bamford Smith from Heston to Llanbedr. He was to 'drone the Firefly Mk 5 into the Smith's Mk 9 autopilot' and therefore needed to have first-hand experience of the Firefly's flight characteristics. Flying with Dickie Dickenson and Alan Grummitt, Bamford Smith soon appreciated the Firefly's 'alarming divergent instability' in certain descending turns. After more trials at Heston and having overcome the 'cross coupling in the autopilot' by 'phase advance in one of the black boxes', Bamford Smith returned to Llanbedr with the first Mk 9 autopilots to introduce the differences.

At RAF Valley No.6 Joint Services Trials Unit was formed to carry out trials with the Fair Fire flash-guided weapon and thus the foundations were laid for the three-way collaboration between Valley, Llanbedr and Aberporth that would see out the century and beyond.

The first air-launch of a fully guided and controlled Firestreak air-to-air missile took place on 5th September 1955 over the Aberporth Range. The missile, launched from a de Havilland Venom, destroyed the unmanned radio-controlled Firefly target operated from Llanbedr. Flight trials then continued at Woomera where the Jindivik was to be the target and CAC Sabres were modified to carry Firestreak. A Hawker Hunter and an English Electric Canberra were also used during these Firestreak trials.

Sergeants' Mess Christmas party, 1955.

The lessons learned during the development of Britain's first operational air-to-air guided missile were invaluable for subsequent missile systems such as Red Top, Sea Slug, Sea Dart, Martel, Sky Flash and Sea Eagle. Later it was claimed that the 85 per cent success rate over a large number of firings by the RAF and the Royal Navy, put Firestreak far in advance of any other missile of this kind.

This was the year that another memorable Llanbedr personality – Gwyn L 'Harlech' Jones – joined the ground staff and went on to become one of the 'pioneers' who would also serve in Australia.

1956

In April Leading Aircraftman Gordon Brown arrived at Llanbedr to do his national service but stayed on to see out the century as Head of Ground Electronics in the Control Tower. John W Andrews (avionics) and Phil Williams also began long-term careers at Llanbedr during this year. Phil would see out the century as Senior Technical Officer.

While Short Brothers continued to service the Fireflies, changes were afoot. Squadron Leaders Sean Scanlon and Ian Popey left.

Flight Lieutenant Pat Collins arrived but then it was decided that the Target Aircraft Service should be civilianised. Mr B H Bryan replaced the RAF Commanding Officer to become the first Officer-in-Charge of RAE Llanbedr, with Gordon Holloway as Senior Administration Officer.

In May, Edwyn Lewis of Harlech, employed in the Motor Transport section, went flying for the first time when Nick Carter (the Manager) offered him 'a flying job' as a Target Towing Operator in Mosquito TT.35s. Edwyn flew in a Mosquito piloted by Don Reed to the Ty Croes firing range on Anglesey. He went on to fly with No.5 CAACU pilots Bob Barnes, Norman Sharp, Veronica Volkersz, Danny Kay, Jack Forster, Johnny Watson, 'Rocky' Oliver, Jock Skinner, Mike Higgins and Arthur 'Wiggy' Wignal.

'Rocky was the pilot when we were struck by lightning, which was very frightening and afterwards the aircraft was out of commission for three months. Another time, when flying with Danny Kay, the Range started firing and although the towed target was 5,500 feet behind us, Danny had to inform the

Edwyn Lewis (right) and Rigger/Winchman Eddie Edwards with the centreline winch on a Mosquito of 5 CAACU at Llanbedr, 1956.

Range Controller, "I'm pulling this target, not pushing it!"' recalled Edwyn. He also remembered the time when Mike Higgins, who had a dinner date that evening, was detailed for a late afternoon sortie for the Tonfannau Range. After a couple of firing runs Mike turned back to Llanbedr, instructing Edwyn to winch in the tow ready to drop it at base before landing. But then Llanbedr Air Traffic Controller Budrewicz passed a message requesting Mike's Mosquito to return to the Range until 6pm:

'Who said I was to stay on range till 1800?'
'Mr Nick Carter, SBH Manager.'
'Tell Nick to get off his fat a*** and come up here and do it himself.'

There was a pause and then: 'Yes Mike. I'll do it next time,' said the Manager over the radio! Mike and Edwyn flew back to Tonfannau for a while and once again Mike instructed Edwyn to start winching in the tow. He apologised to the Controller saying that his aircraft had gone unserviceable and they were returning to base. However, as they taxied in at Llanbedr, they saw another Mosquito being towed out of the hangar. 'What's up with your aircraft? You're to carry on in that one now!' Mike was informed by the Duty Groundcrew Chief.

'After we climbed into the other Mossie, Mike was furious and the air was blue,' remembered Edwyn. 'However, we did complete the programme this time!'.

'Rocky' Oliver and Observer SAC Dave Armitage had a close call on 15th October when their Firefly developed engine trouble during an approach to land at Llanbedr. With wheels and landing flaps down, the Firefly dropped onto hard rough ground at Dyffryn. The fuel tanks ruptured and there was a fire. Dave was knocked unconscious. Rocky extricated Dave but each suffered burns in the process. Rocky's action earned him a George Medal and local man Goronwy Wynn Davies, who'd hurried to help with the rescue, was awarded a Certificate of Commendation. By coincidence, Goronwy was starting work at Llanbedr airfield on the following day! Thirty-six years later, when he retired from his position as MT Chargehand Fitter, Goronwy's colleagues said he would always be remembered for going to the rescue and for his cheerfulness and clean jokes.

During 1956 the Jindivik trials in Australia showed a marked improvement. The malfunction loss rate dropped to 1 in 13 sorties out of the 120 that were carried out. One other aircraft was destroyed by a direct hit from a missile. 'We learned that it was wrong to operate on the basis that, because no human life was at stake, one could take shortcuts and reduce quality control standards in unmanned aircraft,' said Ian. 'The standard had to be higher because there was no human pilot aboard to monitor and take control if necessary.'

While the flight trials sorted out the performance, handling and operational characteristics of the Jindivik, the team also designed the extras to make it an effective target for the evaluation and development of guided weapons. These 'extras' were the enhancement of radar area, augmentation of infrared output and the means for measuring the 'miss distance' of missiles.

At Llanbedr the well-established Firefly drone target service continued to launch from Runway 24, which was 4,656 feet in length while Runway 16 (4,207 feet), with its arrester equipment, was used for landings. Target drones were always escorted by one of the ex-Royal Navy Firefly T.7s (piloted) to the 'gate' to the range. During the sortie the 'Shepherd' held clear and then accompanied the drone back to Llanbedr. While airborne the Firefly drone produced a blip on the radar but there was no telemetry so the Shepherd pilot confirmed commands and altitude changes.

1957

In late January Llanbedr took delivery of its first Meteor U.15 (VT110). Originally built as an F.4, the aircraft had been converted to U.15 configuration by Flight Refuelling Ltd at Tarrant Rushton airfield. The autopilot and associated drone equipment were installed wherever space could be found. The Meteor U.15 could be flown with or without a pilot, as could the later Meteor U.16s (converted F.8s). This enabled Drone Controller training to be carried out with a safety pilot in the cockpit who could disengage auto-control and pilot the aircraft himself. The Meteor drones were not designed to tow targets (a Meteor TT.20 was available for this purpose) but, like the Fireflies, were used for air-to-air Fireflash weapons trials. The Meteor U.16 had a better performance and the control

systems, autopilot and radio equipment were installed in the nose section.

Now under the Ministry of Supply, training on the Meteors began with the RAF pilots from Farnborough while Short Brothers provided the aircraft servicing, civilian pilots and ground controllers.

As civilians took over from the RAF, another notable personality arrived at Llanbedr. RAF-trained Instrument Fitter Mervyn George Hobbs started work in the Drone Instruments Section on 1st April. However in the first five months he also logged 61 flights on his secondary duty as a Flight Test Observer in Fireflies. His debut in the Firefly was to prove memorable, as he recalled: 'On my first flight I made the mistake of asking the pilot (Macdonald) how fast the aircraft could go and when he showed me I left my breakfast in Brian Axworthy's helmet.' Forty-three years later, George saw out the century at Llanbedr in the dual role of Engineering and Contract Manager.

Another long-serving 'George' began his Llanbedr career in 1957 as an electrician. He was 'George' B G Brown. Ron Telfer, Des Roberts and Chris R Smith also began their long-term careers at Llanbedr during 1957.

During April, pilot Veronica Volkersz joined No.5 CAACU at Llanbedr. She was well qualified, having been an Air Transport Auxiliary Flight Captain during World War Two, and a post-war charter pilot who had continued to fly with the RAFVR. She had over 60 aircraft types in her log including fighters and multi-engined bombers. Veronica was the first British woman to fly a jet, when she ferried a Meteor F.4 (EE386) from Moreton Valence to Molesworth. At Llanbedr Veronica mostly flew a Mosquito on target-towing tasks or on fighter control sorties for the RAuxAF. Among Veronica's friends were Elsie and her husband, pilot Arthur 'Danny' Kay. Elsie remembered most of their time at Llanbedr as one long party:

'One year we counted 28 nights' partying on the run, followed by a sixpenny night in the Mess. Brandy and ginger cost sixpence and the buffet was free! I really enjoyed living in Harlech – and the social life! We watched them make the film "Red Beret" with Alan Ladd on the airfield. I learned to drive a car

on the runways when there was no flying on Sundays. Veronica used to fly in formation with my husband and the other pilots in the Battle of Britain air displays. They were all daredevils and used to fly under bridges!'

A new runway, 7,000 feet in length and with approach and landing paths over the sea, was under construction. Around this time a RAuxAF pilot named Eric Ainsworth arrived to fly manned and unmanned Fireflies and Meteors at Llanbedr. The target aircraft were needed for the Thunderbird, Firestreak, Fireflash and Bloodhound missiles (code-named 'Red Shoes', 'Blue Jay', 'Blue Sky' and 'Bloodhound' respectively) that were being developed. The ten Supermarine Swift F.7s of the Guided Weapons Development Squadron, formed at RAF Valley in June 1957 under the control of the Central Fighter Establishment, carried Fireflash; later the unit re-equipped with Gloster Javelin FAW.7s for Firestreak trials.

In Australia, during the summer, the first Meteor U.15 drone flight was made by VT187 from RAAF Evetts Field, Woomera. During the flight the aircraft was hit by the missile. Control was lost and the aircraft dived into the ground on fire. On the next sortie, VW275 fared better and returned to be landed safely.

At Llanbedr Captain Targett-Adams RN (Ret'd), joined Short Brothers as Technical Superintendent and completed the civilianisation process. The Aircraft Engineering Section acquired an Air/Ground Radio Section

The quarry face where Sergeant Bob Barnes died when Meteor F.8 WA794 crashed.

and the Autopilot Section. RAE Farnborough retained the responsibility for 'Inspection'. By the end of the year No.5 CAACU was dispatched to Woodvale due to concerns about operating both unmanned target aircraft and manned aircraft from Llanbedr simultaneously. Dennis Rossell recorded that No.5 CAACU had flown a total of 11,137 hours 55 minutes during their time at Llanbedr, an achievement regrettably marred by the one fatal accident. After an early morning take-off in Meteor F.8 WA794 on 11th October, Sergeant Bob Barnes collided with a quarry face on the seaward side of the Yr Eifl range (commonly known as The Rivals) on the Lleyn Peninsula while flying in low cloud.

During the year, Bamford Smith returned to Llanbedr with an RAE contract to 'integrate with the Firefly technicians and sort out teething troubles' and brought his family to Harlech. Eric Ainsworth became Chief Pilot and a controller of pilotless Fireflies. Stores Officer Charlie Harris began his scrapbook of news cuttings to record life and death at Llanbedr for the next 20 years.

The year also saw a change of title for the airfield as RAF Llanbedr became RAE Llanbedr. It was also the year in which the Sergeants' Mess finally closed. Losing this 'oasis' on 'dry' Welsh Sundays was keenly felt by the local people as well as the airfield staff!

1958

Change, success and near disaster were the keynotes of 1958. Civilianisation went on, the new long runway was completed, the first Meteor drone target sortie took place for a Thunderbird missile – and a manned drone Meteor crashed into two hangars!

In April Mr A P Goode arrived from HQ at Bramshot to become Officer-in-Charge while the establishment was being reorganised. In the same month Robert 'Bob' Gaskell (an RAFVR General Duties pilot during World War Two and an RAuxAF GD pilot afterwards) arrived to become a trials test pilot and a Drone Target Controller at Llanbedr. Bob had served in 611 (West Lancashire) Squadron, RAuxAF at Hooton Park with Eric Ainsworth and the two worked together at Llanbedr for the next 30 years.

The radar system used for tracking and control of drone targets, previously maintained and operated by RAF personnel, 'was placed in the safe hands of Ray Tyson', remembered Derek Whitehead, adding: 'Shortly thereafter the radar system was complemented by an additional MZPI and a further SCR 584. At this point in time a division occurred between Air Traffic and Target Control, the latter suffering the indignity of a remote display called a Skiatron and two home-built remote plan position indicators.'

On 17th July Eric Ainsworth taxied out in the first Meteor U.15 drone to fly a target sortie from Llanbedr. He set the switches, climbed out, closed the canopy and walked away. Shepherd pilot Flight Lieutenant Evan Vigor was already airborne in the Meteor T.7 to escort the target to the Range. Master Controller Peter Pennie gave the go-ahead. Steered by Jimmy James the pilotless Meteor U.15 (RA432) rolled down the runway, lifted off and the gear retracted. It was flown out into Cardigan Bay by Skipper 'Rocky' Oliver and Navigator Bob Gaskell to be 'presented' for the firing. However the 'Red Shoes' missile had become unserviceable so RA432 was brought back to base. Pitch Controller Jack Forster and Azimuth Controller Pilot Officer J James landed it safely after a sortie of 33 minutes.

The next six sorties went well and during the rest of the year's drone Meteor flying only one aircraft was lost. This was Meteor U.15 VT135 that was presented at 30,000 feet for a Sea Slug missile on 18th December. During the return to base when 'land-glide' was selected, the aircraft suddenly dived into the sea and was destroyed.

With Jindivik soon to be operated from Llanbedr, Flight Lieutenant Jack Ramsay arranged for a party of Shorts personnel to visit Melbourne and Woomera in September. They needed to learn about the con-

Wrecked Firefly drones at Llanbedr.

struction, maintenance and operation of the Jindivik Pilotless Target Aircraft, manufactured by GAF in Melbourne, with its British components being the Bristol Siddeley Viper turbojet, the autopilot equipment and other electronic parts.

There was a near-disaster at Llanbedr on Friday 5th September towards the end of a sortie when Meteor U.15 RA415 was being flown in drone configuration, with 'Johnny' F C Johnson as safety pilot. The purpose of the flight had been to prove the drone airborne equipment. Under remote radio control the aircraft had taken off and flown the circuit, followed by a satisfactory approach and overshoot. During a further circuit the pilot took manual control of the throttles although the aircraft was still under radio control. Suddenly, on the final approach, the aircraft yawed and banked steeply to port. The lower wing-tip hit the roof of a Bellman hangar and then the aircraft struck the ground violently. Breaking up, as it went, the out-of-control Meteor thrust its way through the side of a Besseneaux hangar. Amazingly, since he was not wearing a protective helmet, the pilot survived the crash although he suffered severe injuries. However, he eventually recovered and returned to flying as an airline pilot.

At first it seemed that the accident must have been caused by the failure of the port engine, but this did not fit a witness account of a sudden and vicious roll to port. Yaw, followed by roll, was expected with an engine failure. It transpired that five weeks earlier, flying at 800 feet, this Meteor U.15 suddenly dropped the port wing. With enough height available the pilot was able to take over and recover. The roll unit was therefore suspect and was returned to the makers to be stripped down. A new one was fitted to the aircraft and it was assumed the problem was solved. Eventually it was decided that only a defective roll unit in the radio-controlled autopilot could have caused full port aileron to be applied at such a high rate and so the roll unit was redesigned.

On 23rd September Arthur Pearcy, an aviation historian in his spare time, visited Llanbedr: 'The base of the unique ATC tower was littered with wrecked Firefly drones and the dump near one of the hangars revealed a crashed Meteor U.15.' This did not deter Arthur and his wife Audrey from joining the staff as ATC assistants when the Ministry of Supply took over responsibility for Air Traffic Control at Llanbedr on 1st November.

Firestreak, the first British air-to-air missile, had entered service on RAF Javelin FAW.7s during the year and went on to equip all marks of the English Electric Lightning

The remains of Meteor U.15 RA415 after it ploughed into Llanbedr's Besseneaux hangar.

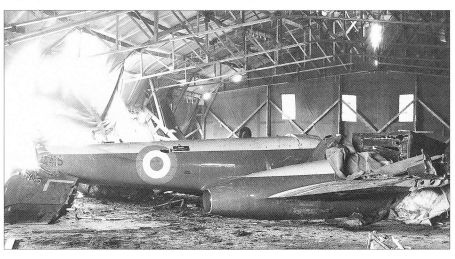

fighter and also the Royal Navy's de Havilland Sea Vixen FAW.1s. Dave Lumb, Sim Oakley, Keith W Unwin and W Tudur Rowlands arrived during the year to begin their long-term careers in the hangars at Llanbedr.

1959

On 1st January a Bloodhound Mk 1 Trials Squadron, parented by RAF North Coates in Lincolnshire, was permanently detached to the RAF Guided Weapons Range Unit (GWRU) at RAF Aberporth and although the name, ownership and status changed numerous times, Llanbedr provided targets for this unit for the next 25 years. In 1984 the unit was disestablished and the Bloodhound equipment and personnel deployed to the front line to carry out firings as detachments from operational squadrons.

A unique Meteor U.15, VT196, was delivered to Llanbedr on 27th February to be turned into the 'Meteorvik' – a Meteor drone with a Jindivik autopilot. Development flight trials were needed to test the special aerials and to prove the telemetry and remote-controlled throttle systems, fitted by Boscombe Down technicians. Then the 'Meteorvik' began the task of preparing everyone at Llanbedr for Jindivik. A new control tower was built and supplied with data from two SCR 584 and one MZPI radar systems until the commissioning of the Decca ASR1 radar.

Meanwhile the target service had provided 60 Meteor U.15 sorties for Sea Slug, Bloodhound and Firestreak missiles. On its first presentation VT338 was shot down by a Bloodhound surface-to-air missile. One of the Meteor drones failed to 'fuel off' on landing and overran the runway and another was damaged on landing. RA442 was shot down over the sea on 23rd April and RA373 suffered the same fate on 4th May.

The Royal Navy was still also using Firefly U.9s (converted Mk 4/5s) but on 20th May Meteor U.15 VT110 was delivered to Llanbedr for the conversion training of the Fleet Air Arm pilots of 728 (B) Squadron from Hal Far, Malta. After starting them off, Llanbedr provided technical support and on occasion loaned aircraft until the Malta pilotless target unit was established.

The first overseas buyer/user of Jindivik was the Royal Swedish Air Force Board which acquired ten Jindivik Mk 2s for their Lapland missile base. Robot Forsoksplats Norland (Missile Testing Range North) Vidsel, close to the Arctic Circle, offered almost 24-hour daylight in the summer months, stable weather conditions and excellent visibility during long midwinter nights undisturbed by artificial light sources. The Jindivik controllers were a team of Swedair pilots who were sent to Llanbedr and learned to fly drones using the 'Meteorvik'. Between 1959 and 1964 the Swedes flew 104 Jindivik sorties in very extreme conditions at Vidsel and lost nine of the ten Jindiviks. They named each Jindivik after a Viking – Tvartra, Tor, Skallagrim etc – and painted a reindeer logo onto each fin.

Summer 1959 was one of the best, weather-wise, when ex-RAF pilot Alec O'Connor arrived for a job interview, the airlines being in recession. 'A night at The Vic, an hour with Nick Carter, the Manager and a chat with Chief Pilot Eric Ainsworth and my fate was happily sealed with a job. Naively I thought that accommodation wouldn't be a problem, but with the Welsh holiday season everywhere was booked for months. Peter Pennie was in the same boat and for the first week we ended up in an establishment we called "Hungry Hall". I had never before seen half a sausage on my breakfast plate or a solitary cracker with a wafer-thin slice of cheese serving as a separate course. Needless to say, The Vic was our second home for refills and drinks served by the urbane Harry Warburton and his staff.'

Alec found digs with Mr and Mrs Arthur at the north end of the village and was soon airborne in a Meteor, refamiliarising with RAF Training Officer Evan Vigar. 'In that blistering summer the sands beyond the aerodrome became a favourite picnic spot. We'd drive out of the back gate at weekends and set up camp – something the land-owner probably didn't know! Walking was painful on the hot sand but the sea temperature was ideal. Among the regulars for these outings were fellow pilots Johnny Watson and Mike Noad, Jack Forster, and his wife Sylvia; and there was an Irish couple, Chris and Ann White.'

Above: **Jindivik operations at Vidsel Missile Base in Lapland.**

Left: **Swedish Jindivik TVÄRTRÄ receives the reindeer logo after its 7th sortie.**

Alec O'Connor spent his first flying hours at Llanbedr in Meteor U.15 VT196. He remembered the aircraft as being 'ancient, vibrating and excruciatingly cold ... like an icebox at high altitude and its gyro instruments precessed at rates which would have staggered their manufacturers!' In the coming months Alec also learned the arcane art of target preparation and controlling.

The Fireflies were heading for retirement, apart from two 'immaculate hacks' used to ferry crews to Tarrant Rushton for aircraft pick-ups. All the targets were now Meteor U.15s. These aircraft were perfectly serviced in immaculately clean hangars, in the charge of 'Ross' and were 'streets ahead' of anything Alec had experienced in the RAF. Alec remembered with affection the Meteor drone operations at Llanbedr:

'No matter how great one's experience, there was an undefinable thrill when, on the take-off command, the two Rolls-Royce Derwents opened up and the pilotless Meteor accelerated down the runway to rotate, lift off, clean itself off and disappear to the Range. The Meteor would be recovered onto the downind leg where, at 1,200 feet above the sea, it would automatically assume "slow-level" configuration at 170 knots with one-third flap. The aircraft was vectored onto the final approach and the landing configuration commanded. When the Pitch and Azimuth Controllers, peering through graticuled binoculars, reported "On Target" the "Cell" handed them control to guide the aircraft to touchdown. The Pitch Controller was responsible for sending a "Fuel Off" signal when he was sure that the Meteor, automatically maintaining 135 knots, would touch down on the runway. As the signal did literally what its name implied the choice of the exact moment was quite critical.

'Crosswind landings could be damaging for friendly relationships because all turn commands involved bank. The Azimuth Controller sometimes had to inject a substantial drift-killing turn just as the Pitch Controller was congratulating himself on a neat roundout. The Pitch Controller then had to do some quick fingerwork to prevent a one-wheel landing or a one-wing-low touchdown!'

During 1959, John S Jones joined the groundcrew team in the Meteor Hangar and saw out the century at Llanbedr.

In Australia on 8th October, the first Jindivik Mk 2 flew, achieving a useful ceiling of 54,000 feet. Seventy-six Mk 2s were built to accommodate the Viper ASV8 turbojet with a thrust of 1,750 lb. They could be fitted with 40-inch wing extensions for high-altitude operations and carried the Mk 4 pods containing the latest 'fish-eye' lens compact cameras. Ian Fleming moved to the head office of the Australian Department of Supply and Tom Shelton enthusiastically took over the development of Jindivik target systems.

During 1959, No.1 Guided Weapons Trials Squadron at Valley was tasked to carry out the in-service trials of the Firestreak Weapon System. Using the six Gloster Javelin FAW.7s on strength the telemetry-proving trials began. There was good cause to celebrate the Christmas break as the first firing took place on 21st December and successfully destroyed the Meteor drone target presented by Llanbedr.

Firefly targets were also still providing a target service and when the Royal Canadian Navy aircraft carrier HMCS *Bonaventure* arrived in Cardigan Bay, six Fireflies were presented. The carrier's McDonnell F2H-3 Banshee fighters, each equipped with two AIM-9 Sidewinder air-to-air missiles, took a substantial toll of the Firefly force!

Stores Officer Charlie Harris recorded the death of Llanbedr fitter Harry Webb shortly after the Canadians' visit – whether or not there was any connection between those events went unrecorded! Nor did Charlie record that during the year George Hobbs, then in his twenties, had begun to make his mark by becoming a Supervisor. On the eve of the first decade of the record-breaking Jindivik at Llanbedr, George took charge of the Jindivik flight control system and set up an autopilot test facility in readiness.

Two of the last Firefly drones at Llanbedr.

Chapter Four

The 1960s

The first 16 Jindiviks arrived in the UK as complete aircraft, but thereafter Fairey Engineering Ltd installed the engines and control items at Ringway in Lancashire. The first Jindivik was brought to Llanbedr by road on 4th January and was ready for engine runs on 3rd March. Eventually BAC Filton in Avon and subsequently the Cranfield Institute of Technology in Bedfordshire became the design authority for Jindivik.

In March Llanbedr's OC Flying Flight Lieutenant H J Dodgson flew to Malta to observe the first pilotless flight of the Royal Navy Meteor U.15 target drone VT110 and to see Llanbedr's protégées aboard the Guided Missile Trials ship HMS *Girdle Ness* shoot it out of the sky with a Sea Slug missile. At Llanbedr Meteor U.15 VZ415 survived its thirtieth sortie which was also the 100th Meteor U.15 drone flight.

The first UK Jindivik (A92-106) took off under remote control at 6.20pm on 26th April. This gave the operating crew some experience of handling the Jindivik at medium altitude and the opportunity to check the instrumentation. The conclusions were favourable except for the poor telemetry display when the fuel registered at 40 gallons and the Shepherd pilots Eric Ainsworth and F C Johnson having to ask for the Jindivik's rpm to be reduced so they could keep up! The Master Controller's responsibilities went to Flight Lieutenants H J Dodgson and Evan Vigar with Flight Lieutenant Peter Pennie in the Skipper's seat. Bob Gaskell was the Navigator, backed up by Mike Noad. Out on the airfield Jack Forster was Pitch Controller, accompanied by T J 'Pat' Bolger and Alec O'Connor was the Azimuth Controller, accompanied by W Bill Simms. Alec recalled some of the problems they faced when working with the new drone:

'For Sight operators, the main problem was the Jindivik's diminutive size. The Meteor was easier to spot in poor visibility. You could see which way the nose was pointing and

Jindivik A92-106 is prepared for the first UK Jindivik flight, 26th April 1960.

the angle of bank in time for landing. But often one could see only the Jindivik's nose-light and controlling a light was far more difficult than controlling an aeroplane.'

On one of the early sorties someone increased the sensitivity of the elevator control and the Jindivik performed wild and diverging pitch oscillations as it neared the runway. After the Master Controller gave the overshoot command and the Jindivik came around for a second approach, Alec was astonished to hear that the sensitivity was to be further increased and warned: 'If you do that it will result in a g-stall on one of the pull-outs!' They were prophetic words. On the next approach ("finals" in more sense than one) the oscillations became even more spectacularly divergent, and the Jindivik could take no more, flicking onto its back and crashing into the dune.'

After the first few take-offs, George Hobbs (in consultation with colleagues Sim Oakley and Stan Robinson) redesigned the trolley guidance system. Their modified trolley worked well on being pushed up and down in the hangar. However, they wanted to test it at a higher speed and persuaded Bill Jones from the Telemetry section to tow it on Runway 24 with his beloved Sunbeam Talbot while George sat on the trolley. When they reached top speed, George released the towrope and thus they proved their new guidance system!

Gradually the Jindivik was subjected to more demanding trials. On 22nd June, control problems were experienced and in spite of the efforts of the operating crew and technicians, they could not be resolved before the Jindivik ran out of fuel. So they turned it out to sea and ditched it.

Meteor U.15 target operations mostly went smoothly, with little of the excitement and anxiety of the old Firefly pilotless sorties. So, when the first Meteor U.16 (WH284) arrived in June, the Firefly era was over and the last drone Firefly, U.8 WJ147 'Cuckoo in the Nest' flew gracefully into the sea. The pilot of the shepherding aircraft was observing the behaviour of his charge so closely that he nearly followed it into the sea!

Meteor U.16 WH284 was destroyed on its third sortie by a Firestreak missile, but the

George Hobbs, Sim Oakley and Stan Robinson redesigned the Jindivik take-off trolley guidance system.

next U.16 to arrive (WK926) achieved several 'firsts'. It flew the first pilotless Meteor sortie on 12th September and reached 200 sorties by mid-November. On 24th November it was the first drone to conduct a trial at 40,000 feet and was also the first drone to be landed by the Skipper from the Control Cell, aided by Precision Approach Radar (PAR).

The Meteor U.16s were converted from Meteor F.8s and the pilots found them smoother and more comfortable to fly. The canopy slid closed at the push of a button while pressurisation and cockpit heating worked well. In the Meteor U.15 the autopilot and allied drone equipment were installed wherever space permitted whereas structural alterations were made to the U.16 to improve the aircraft's flexibility as a target without degrading its performance. Radio control and autopilot equipment were housed in the extended nose with a hinged door for access. There was an extra fuel tank in the fuselage and wing-tip nacelles carried cameras that could be jettisoned and recovered from the sea.

As in the Jindivik, the Signal Fail Orbit system would fly the drone to a safety altitude of 5,000 feet to orbit until the signal was restored. Again like the Jindivik, Command Destroy caused the drone to dive steeply into the sea. Telemetry systems provided the Control Cell with performance and navigational information. Extra trials equipment could be fitted under the wings, including flares to provide an infra-red source.

Twice, pilotless Meteor targets suddenly dived into the sea from the base leg turn. As no explanation for these sudden manoeuvres could be found, Navy divers examined the aircraft where they lay on the bottom of the sea. They found the elevators fully down on each of the wrecked Meteors, just as if the 'DESTROY' command had been sent. Investigations found that the radio transmissions of a Dublin taxi firm activated the 'DESTROY' system by some freakish mischance! To prevent repetition an infallible discrete radio command system was introduced. Years later I learned that the Australians had a similar problem which led to an altitude limitation of 35,000 feet on their Jindivik flying. The Australians noted that this was '... due to one of our tele frequencies clashing with a Melbourne radio taxi company. Apparently we either jam out their signals or tell the driver to go to the wrong address!'

One day an unmanned Meteor U.16 target (WF741) was 'misbehaving' after a firing sortie. Shepherd pilot Alec O'Connor found it 'flying at high speed with everything down, and a large hole through the rear fuselage. The crew got it safely down at Llanbedr and we found the missile had entered the fuselage, careered along destroying various control channels and made its exit fractionally before the fuselage fuel tank. It had carried away the airspeed sensor, so that the throttles were fully open as it manfully tried to increase the airspeed from apparent zero. When I saw the damage I thought that I would never have flown so close to an unmanned aircraft if I had known!'

On another occasion the weather deteriorated but the remaining fuel permitted only two attempts to land the Meteor drone (WK926). Alec explained what happened next: 'With visibility less than 150 metres, Azimuth was hastily removed from the

Pilotless Meteor after '...flying at high speed with everything down and a large hole...'.

Recovering an early Jindivik fitted with a calibration mirror to measure wing-flexing.

upwind end of the runway. As a PAR approach was started the Pitch Controller was briefed to give the "Fuel Off" if he saw the Meteor in anything like a suitable position for landing. On the first attempt he saw nothing and the Meteor was sent around. On the final attempt the PAR controller and the Cell Crew used all their combined skills to achieve a stabilised approach and this time the Pitch Controller heard the approaching aircraft. He saw a grey shape flash past so he pressed "Fuel Off". The next 30 seconds must have been the longest in several people's lives as they waited to see or hear where eight tons of pilotless Meteor had gone!

'Some vehicles began a cautious tour of the runway, still cloaked in thick sea fog. They found the Meteor just off the side of the runway and almost undamaged. The approach was so accurate that the aircraft had only diverged onto the grass because the autopilot system did not have the usual help from the Azimuth Controller.'

The Meteor U.16 in question had been airborne for a record 89 minutes. But this aircraft was to break no more records for it was destroyed by a Firestreak air-to-air missile launched by a Javelin FAW.7 of the Guided Weapon Training Squadron later that day.

By the end of 1960 over 30 Jindivik sorties had been flown from Llanbedr and two more Jindiviks had been lost.

Charlie Harris' record showed that Fireman Evan Richards had died in hospital during the year following an operation.

1961

In February two Jindiviks were shot down and by the end of the year another eight had been destroyed. Two were lost in the approach and landing phase, one stalled onto Harlech beach and another crashed on landing. Llanbedr was learning that Jindivik was a drone with a much smaller target presentation and a flight envelope considerably exceeding that of the Meteor. It also required different operating techniques and, as it could not be conventionally flight-tested, all the settings and adjustments had to be made on the ground.

On 16th March, Flying Officer Daniels made the last Firefly flight in one of the two remaining AS.7s before it went for scrap to Hants & Sussex Aviation Ltd. The arrival of an English Electric Canberra led to a brief strike because there were items that a single pilot could not reach. Civilian pilots were invited to accompany their RAF colleagues to fulfil this lesser role but some refused. The RAF officer in charge of Operations promptly suspended the target service and the dispute was quickly resolved.

At Woomera, when the Viper ASV11 turbojet arrived, with a maximum sea level static thrust of 2,500 lb, the changes required to accommodate the new engine were quickly made and the first Jindivik Mk 3 flew on 12th May. The limitations of the automatic control system held the useful ceiling to around 55,000 feet although there was potential to exceed 60,000 feet. Nine Jindivik Mk 3s were built, closely followed by the Mk 3A variant with a new automatic pilot, an AC system, more versatile radar and infra-red augmentation equipment. Pod development increased fuel capacity as well as accommodating cameras. Also, 80-inch wing extensions for very high altitude operations could be fitted.

In July Llanbedr launched a pilotless Meteor target for Ty Croes to demonstrate the English Electric Thunderbird anti-aircraft gun to an audience of War Office VIPs and foreign military observers including General Jacques Faure, commander of France's anti-aircraft defences. The press reported: 'On the gale-buffeted headland Britain's space-age gunners plotted the end of a yellow Meteor jet fighter at 20,000 feet. The gunners released their khaki-coloured killer and ten seconds later Thunderbird made its kill.'

In August Llanbedr took delivery of A92-207, its first Jindivik Mk 102B. In Australia, the Mark 3A first flew on 10th November. With the 80-inch wing extensions fitted it could operate to 67,000 feet and several times 69,000 feet was reached. To ensure the combustion system would remain alight over the full range of operating conditions, Jindivik became an engine testbed. Relight equipment was fitted and when a flameout occurred the Jindivik was brought down to 25,000 feet for relight and then climbed up

again to repeat the test. Very high altitude operations with an auxiliary rocket motor fitted to a Jindivik Mk 3A were also explored and an altitude of 67,000 feet achieved.

In view of the increasing costs of Jindivik, the contractor, assisted by Pete W Smith from the Ministry of Supply, designed a towed target system with winches. Expendable tows carried flares to provide an infra-red homing source streamed behind the Jindivik in flight. With a winch under each wing, two firings could be carried out on each sortie. Other decoy targets, actively or passively radar-augmented, were also developed.

The Jindivik Mk 3B incorporated some modifications to increase speeds at low level and thus offered the following performance: 500 knots EAS from 50–6,000 feet; Mach 0.86 from 6,000–50,000 feet and Mach 0.72 at 65,000 feet; 60° bank angle up to 60,000 feet; 4g pull-ups from 50 feet; operational ceiling of 67,000 feet and minimum operating height of 50 feet; high-altitude endurance of 112 minutes or a range of 900 nautical miles; operations with or without either 40-inch or 80-inch wing extensions; a choice of small Mk 5 camera pods or large Mk 8 pods (camera + fuel + Luneberg lens).

In November, as there was then no market for large 'warbirds', the last of the Firefly airframes was sawn to pieces. In December 'Father Christmas' (Arthur Pearcy) arrived at the Llanbedr children's Christmas party by air. Watched by 150 local youngsters he was winched onto the airfield from a Whirlwind helicopter, courtesy of RAF Valley.

Clerk of Works Bob Jones died suddenly from a thrombosis and Dai Williams of Motor Transport also died following a long illness during the year, according to Charlie Harris.

A towed target system with winches was designed. Here a tow is being streamed from Jindivik A92-258.

A choice of wing pods plus the 40-inch and 80-inch wing extensions.

Jindivik A92-402 during Jindivik Operations at NAS Point Mugu, California.

1962

Alec O'Connor joined the pilots who left to become Air Traffic Controllers and he went on to become Civil Aviation Authority Head of Licensing Standards. 'None of us will forget those magic moments when a blast of jet wake would shake the Azimuth unit and with a heart-stopping roar the pilotless target would speed down the runway to meet whatever fate awaited out on the range,' said Alec.

After three and a half years flying Meteors at Llanbedr, ex-RAF Hawker Hunter test pilot 'Pat' Bolger also left, to fly for Flight Refuelling Ltd at Tarrant Rushton. Bill Simms, another ex-RAF pilot, also became a civilian Air Traffic Controller after 3½ years flying and operating Meteors and Jindiviks at Llanbedr. In June RAE Llanbedr hosted a gathering of Royal Observer Corps members from the surrounding areas. Welcomed by Flight Lieutenant 'Peter' E F Pennie DFM, the group was looked after by Mr and Mrs Arthur Pearcy who were Radio Officers at RAE Llanbedr and also members of the ROC.

The United States Pacific Missile Range was the next overseas buyer for Jindivik, three Jindivik Mk 3s and a mobile ground station being air-freighted to Naval Air Station Point Mugu, California. However, when the joint Weapons Research Establishment and Royal Australian Air Force team of salesmen/demonstrators took their van, equipment and Jindiviks to RAAF Edinburgh Field for loading onto the American freighter, their

van was found to be too tall to fit in the hold. WRE tradesmen worked all night to cut off the top so that it could be stowed and re-attached on arrival in the US!

Despite this bad start the Jindivik Mk 3s impressed the Americans. One reached an altitude of 60,000 feet, a record height for a pilotless aircraft at that time. On the first landing demonstration the Jindivik ran on and on towards the Batsman standing on the runway, who stuck to his task without flinching as the Jindivik slid inexorably on, coming to rest with the pitot head accurately aligned on his midriff and comfortably within hand-shaking distance. As one of the Americans commented: 'I told you they could bring them right back!'

It was rare for unmanned aircraft to be allowed to land back at such a base but the team was determined to break into the US market, so Jindiviks were flown in condi-tions made difficult by fog and with the threat of being cut down if the drone strayed from the planned flight path or if visibility closed in. After 14 sorties the US Navy acquired 42 Jindivik Mk 3As to operate from San Nicholas Island, about 75 miles south-west of Los Angeles. They supported this 'notable pro-gram of a jet-powered pilotless aircraft being launched from a three-wheel dolly' with instrumentation radar, photo-theodolites, telemetry, radio command control, aircraft fuel, a 'display van' for observers and a hold-back device for the runway.

Jindivik A92-402 climbs away from the runway at NAS Point Mugu. Note the Royal Australian Air Force roundel.

Another Jindivik landing at NAS Point Mugu. Note the mission marks on the upper forward fuselage.

More Jindiviks had been shot down in Cardigan Bay by July when George Hobbs flew to Australia to arrange the purchase of Jindivik Mk 3As for Llanbedr. Bloodhound and Firestreak missiles, Javelins, Lightnings and Royal Navy gunfire were all taking their toll. In September a Jindivik disappeared from Aberporth Range radar cover, causing concern until it was re-identified – over the Bristol Channel! To avoid flying back over land the Jindivik was destroyed at sea.

The numerous railway crossings between Barmouth and Penrhyndeudrath claimed another victim in early December when Tommy Atkins, a rigger at the airfield, was killed by a train at Llanaber.

1963

Over 300 Jindivik flights had been achieved when the first two shootdowns of the year occurred in February. A further two Jindiviks were destroyed in March for safety reasons and ten more were shot down by 24th June when a Jindivik Mk 102B (A92-248) was launched on its fourth sortie. After half-an-hour's flying the Jindivik was in the circuit to land, but failed to turn starboard onto Ground Controlled Approach finals and then rolled to the left. The Jindivik hit the hillside three miles north of Porthmadog, a small fire breaking out on impact. The press reported: 'There were no casualties and no damage to property when the pilotless plane crashed about a quarter of a mile from Gesail Farm, Cwmstradllyn, near Porthmadog.'

Development trials with towed target systems were successful. There was an aerodynamically shaped body containing a pack of infra-red flares with a winch fitted to the aircraft in a 'shoe' that also acted as a stowing point for the target before streaming. A conductor wire formed the core of the target-towing cable and carried the electrical current to fire the infra-red flares. For radar homing weapons a similar towed body containing a Luneberg lens was used. With the towed target trailing behind and below the Jindivik the separation mostly ensured the safety of the target aircraft as well as giving accurate miss-distance scoring.

Gordon Brown monitors flight data during a pilotless sortie.

1964

Early in the year, Flight Refuelling Ltd completed their one hundredth drone conversion of a Meteor F.8 for the Ministry of Supply. Ninety-two of the drones were to U.16 standard for Llanbedr and eight were to U.21 standard for use at Woomera. The company was also developing a towed target system. Among numerous developments for Jindivik were the wing extensions for high-altitude work, but: 'When we did the rigging for the 80-inch extensions, they were not within the specification,' recalled George Hobbs, 'so we consulted Aussie aerodynamicist Charlie Mulhauser and Project Officer Robin Harper. Both went away to think about it and Charlie returned with some bits of tin to rivet on – it flew like a bird!' Jindivik Mk 102B A92-529 made three flights, reaching an altitude of 60,800 feet on the second, and streaming a towed target at 55,000 feet on the third.

After six years as Officer-in-Charge Mr A P Goode left to join the War Department of the Ministry of Defence (MoD). In recognition of his work at Llanbedr, presentations were made on behalf of Shorts, Aberporth and airfield departments.

The 800th Jindivik sortie took place in the autumn and in November A92-416 was the first Jindivik Mk 103A at Llanbedr. Jindivik sorties during 1964 totalled 341 while Meteor sorties had dwindled to less than 50.

In December Mr C M Rhodes became the new Officer-in-Charge. Charlie Harris' obituary record listed Brian Titterall from the Radio Section (suicide/gunshot), Foreman Evan Griffith Williams (after a long illness), Flight Lieutenant 'Bill' W S Smith AFC (killed in Aden), Accounts Clerk E Denton-Davies (Aintree Hospital) and Stan Wardle (thrombosis while on the Isle of Man).

1965

Four flights in varying pod, fuel and winch configurations were made with Jindivik Mk 103A A92-427, during which the maximum altitude achieved was 62,400 feet while the maximum flight duration was 91 minutes. On 22nd June Llanbedr staff were able to celebrate their achievement when Jindivik A92-259 was landed back from the 1,000th UK Jindivik sortie. Among the year's losses was a Jindivik that 'flamed out' twice over the sea, but would only relight once.

The complete workforce at Evetts Field, Woomera, South Australia. The 'WRE' on the rear fuselage of the Jindivik stands for Weapons Research Establishment.

Charlie Harris recorded that Chief Instrument Engineer Happy Cunningham died suddenly at home, that Bob Hughes and Will Morris (Motor Transport Fitter) died in Bangor and Jack Jones from Dyffryn died from silicosis during the year.

1966

Jindivik A92-436 made a presentation for a Bloodhound missile, reaching 62,000 feet and with a flight time of 65 minutes. In October the Australian government awarded Short Brothers & Harland the contract for the operation and maintenance of the Target Aircraft complex and the Range Ferry and Recovery Flight at RAAF Evetts Field, Woomera. A team from Llanbedr went to Australia to support the Woomera trials.

'What the HELL am I doing' thought Gwyn 'Harlech' Jones as the chartered coach carrying the small group of technicians and their families left Llanbedr airfield, shrouded in misty rain, en route for Woomera. 'An official from Australia House told us of the great advantages of emigration to Australia. We knew we were committed to three years in the Simpson Desert, but we listened courteously although Sim Oakley did enquire: "If it's so great down there, what are you doing HERE?". At Heathrow there was a flurry of uniformed police activity. Ronald Biggs, the Great Train Robber was rumoured to be attempting to fly to Australia that very day. Later events proved he was successful!

'On landing at Perth we learned sadly of the Aberfan disaster. Via Adelaide we went to Woomera and then to RAAF Evetts Field for our first working day. We were to integrate with the Royal Australian Air Force operation and build up a civilian company to take over. The first phase was easily achieved mainly due to our leader, Captain Targett-Adams.

'Having contributed to the greater part of 1,348 Jindivik flights at Llanbedr there was some tongue in my cheek when my RAAF mentors pronounced that "Mr G L Jones, having undergone a course of instruction by the RAAF, is competent to carry out the duties of Strip Engineer". My colleagues asked if we'd continue to hear "She's apples, mate" and "Give her a kick and she'll be right" or "Good on yer, blue" on the r/t!

'Our families integrated well. Our soccer team "The Rovers", managed by the late Ivor Williams of Blaenau Ffestiniog, went on to win the Woomera Soccer Championship and Woomera Cup double in 1968, 1969 and 1970.'

Captain Targett-Adams stayed on in Australia and Wing Commander 'Tommy' Atkins took over as Technical Superintendent for Short Brothers & Harland at Llanbedr, becoming Manager in 1967.

It was an eventful year with three Jindivik crashes on land. In April, after take-off, a Jindivik climbed too steeply, became inverted, stalled and burned out on the airfield. Then in September, Jindivik A92-448 failed to turn onto the final approach or to respond to the 'DESTROY' command. To the surprise of a retired policeman and his family from Norwich, who were driving along the B4391 from Bala to Ffestiniog, the Jindivik suddenly appeared low above the ground and heading towards them! Clearing a stone wall it bounced on the roof of their car and crashed into the hillside at Pont Afon Gan, where it burst into flames. Mr Thomas Robinson and his family were unhurt, so he hurried up the slope intending to help 'the pilot' but learned from the rescue services that there was no-one to rescue. The Jindivik crashed through some power lines so electricity was cut off in the area, '…but the supply was soon restored by MANWEB workmen,' reported *The Liverpool Daily Post*.

Basil Jerram, who took up the post of Chief Engineer in December, arrived at Llanbedr in the middle of the crisis following the crash of Jindivik A92-448. Basil was a professional Civil Service engineer who sought the Llanbedr posting when his work on Blackburn Buccaneer development at Brough diminished. Around this time an annual conference on Target Development was held at Llanbedr. Attended by 20 representatives from Australia, Canada and the USA and led by Brigadier Mills, Director General Weapons (Technical) of the Ministry of Aviation, the group divided its time between the Conference Room and demonstrations of target flying and equipment.

When a fisherman's catch in Cardigan Bay included the waterproof camera from a Jindivik which had been shot down by a missile from an RAF fighter a month previously, this provided a good story for the press: 'The first target aircraft to record its own destruction' and 'Experts have been able to plot the exact path missiles take before hitting their target' were examples of the headlines that appeared. Officer-in-Charge Mr Colin Rhodes told the press: 'The film was intact and shows a missile approaching the aircraft, hitting it and debris flying.'

A month later 'Plans to air-launch American supersonic unmanned targets from Canberra aircraft for guided missile trials in Cardigan Bay' were disclosed at a press conference at RAE Llanbedr. Mr Rhodes revealed that initial steps to receive the Beech AQM-37A supersonic target would begin in two years. This first Open Day for press and TV at RAE Llanbedr was followed by another open day for senior officials of the County of Merioneth. The work of the establishment and the target drones was demonstrated on both days. Just before Christmas a Jindivik was written off on landing due to a mistake by a trainee Azimuth Controller.

During 1966 the results of a test-bore near RAE Llanbedr revealed that at one time a pebble beach existed close to the road leading to the airfield. 'As the airfield elevation is only 23 feet above sea level it is probable that the airfield was once covered by the waters of Tremadoc Bay. When Harlech Castle was built ships could sail over what is now the local golf course right up to the foot of the castle. Maps only 200 years old show the River Artro flowing over part of what is now the airfield and making a complete island out of Mochras (Shell Island),' it was reported.

Short Brothers' Manager at Llanbedr Mr Thomas D 'Nick' Carter died in hospital on 30th December after a short illness. His Requiem Mass in Barmouth, early in the New Year, brought many local people together with representatives of Short Brothers & Harland, Flight Refuelling Ltd, RAE Farnborough, the Ministry of Technology and the RAF.

1967

The US Navy received its last Jindiviks during 1967 and completed 175 sorties, leaving only one Jindivik serviceable when operations were concluded. The high loss rate was attributed more to missile strikes than malfunctions. However, while the Americans chopped Jindiviks out of the sky, the Royal Australian Navy began operating them from the Jervis Bay Missile Range in New South Wales.

Short Brothers, incorporated in Australia as Messrs Shorts Brothers & Harland Air Services Ltd on 9th January, won the contract to maintain and operate Jindiviks for the Royal Australian Navy and launched the first Jindivik there on 7th February. Gwyn 'Harlech' Jones was detached from Woomera to Jervis Bay along with Royal Australian Air Force personnel to present the inaugural target. The task was 'Range Acceptance Trial, 25,000 feet, max speed 250 knots'. Jindivik N11-496 made this successful first sortie in the hands of: Skipper, Flight Lieutenant Crimmons; Pilot, Squadron Leader Johnston; 'Bats', Flight Lieutenant Hunt and Navigator, Flying Officer Leray-Meyer.

Author's Note: 'Bats' was the term used by our Australian counterparts for what the British called 'Azimuth Controller'. 'Pilot' was their term for our Pitch Controller. The Australians did not have a 'Master Controller' as we did.

At RAAF Evetts Field, the Short Bros takeover from the Royal Australian Air Force led to

another first in June when Jindivik A92-418 was launched for a successful flight in the hands of company staff. The aircraft went on to make 285 flights before being destroyed by a Rapier missile in 1974.

At Llanbedr on 5th October a Jindivik was launched for 19 (F) Squadron, RAF. Pilot Roger Beazley, flying a Lightning, fired his first Firestreak missile at the Jindivik. 'We both got back to base on that occasion,' recalled Roger who fired a number of Firestreak, AIM-9 Sidewinder and AIM-7 Sparrow air-to-air missiles at Jindiviks during his five years on fighter aircraft. But later on 'only one of us got back to base' when Roger downed a Jindivik with a Sparrow missile in a head-on firing while flying a 43 Squadron McDonnell Douglas Phantom FG.1 from RAF Leuchars. Twenty-two years later, Roger was even more interested in Llanbedr when he became Commanding Officer Experimental Flying at RAE Farnborough, with responsibility for some of the Llanbedr operation.

Charlie Harris' record for the year showed that Mr Lewis Jones of Dyffryn, a member of the Security Staff, died of a heart attack.

1968

A news cutting from a March 1968 edition of the *Western Mail* kept by Charlie Harris in his scrapbook reported: '$400,000 Target Plane Deal for BAC – a contract for assembling and testing pilotless aircraft – some of which are shot down over Cardigan Bay as target practice for the RAF – has been awarded to the British Aircraft Corporation's guided-weapons division. The Bristol works has been selected by the Ministry of Technology to assemble and test the latest batch of Jindivik target aircraft, manufactured in Australia and sent to Britain as a bare airframe. The contract includes the manufacture of electronic units and the modification of the aircraft to UK standards.

'The Jindivik system has been used with almost every British surface-to-air guided weapon. The target on a wire tow-line carries signal-enhancing equipment which attracts the missile fired against it leaving the Jindivik unharmed. It has a top speed over 500 mph and can operate from 200 feet to

60,000 feet. Safety systems include a self-destroying device which can be operated by an independent radio link if the normal control link fails.' Charlie noted: 'You can READ all about it, but just try TALKING about it and you will be in the lock-up before you can say Jindivik!'

During the year, Chief Engineer Basil Jerram made his first liaison visit to Australia. He recalled: 'Woomera Range was operational and the traffic between the UK and Australia was considerable so the MoD had a Bristol Britannia on permanent charter. Passengers received a modest form of VIP treatment. We used the tail number "Charlie Foxtrot" as a term of reference and affection. The journey involved overnight stops at fairly luxurious hotels in the Middle East and Singapore (excellent for shopping!) and a refuelling stop in India.'

Back at Llanbedr, Mr A W E Stanley became Officer-in-Charge and George Hobbs was promoted to Deputy Chief Instrument Engineer and given responsibility for Flight and Drone Instruments, Aircraft/Missile Proximity Optical Recorder systems, BAC winch and Towed Target systems and the Rushton tow system.

In August the first live Beech AQM-37C Stiletto firing took place on Aberporth Range. 'Stiletto was an American-designed and manufactured system,' explained Basil Jerram. 'The supersonic target was rocket-propelled and air-launched from its station under the wing of a Canberra and could achieve Mach 2 in straight and level flight.'

In October Avro Anson T.21 VS562 made its final 'flight', being lifted by crane into the compound of 2445 (ATC) Squadron, located just across the road from RAE Llanbedr, to become a source of interest and study for the cadets.

Charlie Harris' list of obituaries for the year included Bob Evans (Dai Photos), Ernest Lloyd 'Ginger' Roberts from Stores (drowned in Cheshire) and G R Williams, a Motor Transport driver from Barmouth.

Pete Pennie at the Master Controller's desk at RAE Llanbedr.

1969

In February Captain R P Targett-Adams RN (Ret'd) died following throat cancer and was buried in the cemetery at Woomera. Shorts were awarded a further three-year contract and 'Jock' Blair, the new Manager, invited Gwyn 'Harlech' Jones to read a feasibility study on the presentation of a supersonic ballistic rocket target service for a secret missile – Sea Wolf. 'It means staying on for another three years. The job's yours and you can pick your own team' Gwyn was told and accepted. He recalled: 'I selected three Aussies and three "poms" and they proved to be superb choices.'

At Llanbedr the 2,000th UK Jindivik sortie was flown on 12th June by A92-437 with Pete Pennie as Master Controller and Bob Gaskell as Skipper. Three days later, RAF Squadron Leader John O'Neill arrived at Llanbedr to become OC Flying for three years, a time he remembered as being 'the happiest, most rewarding and most demanding of my service career. Where else but Llanbedr could one fly six aircraft types in a day: Hunter, Canberra B.2, Meteors T.7, U.16 and TT.20 and the Devon C.2, then throw in an occasional stint as Master Controller for a drone sortie.

'The introduction to my future staff was uncomfortable because, apart from my deputy Flight Lieutenant Colin Westwood, the Flying/Ops people were mature men who had probably seen war service and were long-established in their jobs. They

Marking the 2,000th Jindivik sortie on 12th June 1969.

were civilians and here was a new young boss. What they didn't know was my directive from Farnborough to check and raise (if necessary) and maintain RAF standards of flying and airmanship. Happily, my fears were unfounded.

'The Master Controller had a splendid view of Shell Island from ATC but only a small box of switches and a headset full of recordings from hell! I prayed that I would never have to take control, but I needn't have worried because the boys in the Control Cell were supremely competent and the engineers simply brilliant. I flew regularly with all the pilots and revalidated ex-RAF pilot Peter Shaw as a civilian pilot and converted "Bing" Crosby to the Meteor. I sent both Eric Ainsworth and Bob Gaskell solo in the Hunter, an aircraft many steps ahead of the Meteor.

'In the Ops room there was Bob Hunter chain-smoking, with Derek Newton (who also ran Cae Nest guest-house with his wife Kit) at the comms console, Eric at his desk puffing away at a Hamlet as he did his admin, and people milling around in air so thick with smoke you could cut it with a knife. Griff, our cleaner, tea-maker and barber scraped congealed nicotine off the windows. In the crew-room, each in his own chair, were Bob

Gaskell, Peter Shaw, Ray Gough, Dave Ross, Arthur Guest, Ian Macdonald and then Don Reed. Downstairs the incomparable Peter Pennie occasionally emerged to put the world in order. Llanbedr was a Ministry of Technology, later MoD(PE) establishment so there were Ministry men in charge of various departments.'

The *RAE News* at the time reported: 'There are some Jindiviks at Llanbedr which have each flown a large number of sorties. At present the record stands at 81. However although there have been 2,000 Jindivik TAKE-OFFS, the number of LANDINGS is significantly less! This is because Jindivik is basically a target aircraft.' Was there a connection between this statement and the Chancellor of the Exchequer's visit? Was he checking up on how many of the taxpayers' target aircraft were being brought down by our own side? No! In fact Mr Roy Jenkins MP was en route from Scotland to Aberystwyth to address a Labour Party Rally!

The death of Cleaner Dai (Mable) Jones of Barmouth, from a thrombosis, was noted by Charlie Harris.

Chapter Five

The 1970s

In May 1970 the first Jindivik Mk 103B (A92-619) arrived. The Mk 103A and Mk 103B were versatile, flew at high subsonic speeds and in addition to towed targets could carry a wide variety of trials equipment. Passive radar augmentation to simulate a larger aircraft was achieved by Luneberg lenses in the wing pods and active radar augmentation included traveller-wave tubes and transponders. Luneberg lens positions were varied to suit trials requirements. Visual tracking flares could be carried around the tail pipe, providing the heat source for a close-proximity round. Wing pod cameras provided full photographic coverage around the Jindivik with a mirror system taking in the tow.

Jindivik sorties averaged about 50 minutes' duration, reducing to 35 minutes in a high-speed low-level role. With 40-inch wing extensions fitted an altitude of 57,000 feet or

Jindivik Mk 103B A92-612 sustained damage to its rear fuselage but survived and went on to be shot down on its 35th sortie by an AIM-7 Sparrow air-to-air missile.

more was possible at 270 KTIAS. The clipped-wing version permitted an altitude of 30,000 feet and 440 KTIAS. The option of either 30° or 60° angle of bank (AOB) turns was improved to allow turning from 5° to 60° AOB. Diving manoeuvres were programmed into the autopilot and the radio-altimeter allowed trials to be conducted as low as 50 feet. Ancillary equipment was improved, air and ground systems were duplicated. A signal fail system caused a continuous orbit at a safe height until command was restored and another system allowed for the aircraft to be ditched into the sea.

Charlie Harris recorded that Night Watchman E J Ellis Knight from Llanfrothen had died.

1971

The Ministry of Defence (Procurement Executive) was born with responsibility for procuring sea, land and air weapons systems, defence equipment and for Defence Research and Development. Over the next ten years 'rationalisation' reduced the number of R&D establishments from 25 to 11 accompanied by the rundown of staff. RAE Llanbedr employed 232 people with Shorts Flying Services Division operating the airfield for the Ministry of Defence.

The company magazine *Short Story* covered Llanbedr in 'Operation Phoenix' featuring Wing Commander 'Tommy' Atkins and his Secretary Ann Hughes JP, described as 'the most beautiful beak in Britain'. The article also covered assembly and maintenance of unmanned Jindivik and Meteor target aircraft, the maintenance of those Meteors that were not droned (T.7, NF.11, NF.14 variants and a TT.20 capable of towing a 19,000-foot wire), a Hunter and the Canberra PR.3 (WE146) for Stiletto supersonic targets. They met Chief Aircraft Engineer 'Ross' Rossell, his deputy W J 'Bill the Bee' Jones and secretary Cathy Brown. In Operations they found Chief Pilot Eric Ainsworth and colleagues Bob Gaskell, Peter Shaw, Arthur Guest, David Ross, Ray Gough and Alan Scott. They met Chief Instrument Engineer 'Dusty' Rhodes and his assistant Technical Co-ordinator Carol Ellis, Chief Radio Engineer Ray Tyson, Admin Officer Duncan MacDonald and Technical Photographer Mick Doyle. Following up a Jindivik sortie they saw Gwyllym Owen, in charge of the Jindivik Hangar, preparing the target for flight with Victor Humphries checking the aerial system before Strip Engineer Ken Griffith supervised the radio and instrument checks on the runway. In the Control Cell the team comprised engineer Graham Biswell, Skipper Eric Ainsworth and Navigator Dick Shanks with Hugh Mc Master, Ted Manvell and Ann Giles further along the corridor in the Telemetry Room. Manning the Transmitter Room were Jim Wallace and Mike Fairfax-Rawlings. In the top of the Control Tower they saw Audrey Pearcy, assisting Steve Learoyd, working alongside Master Controller Pete Pennie. Idris Lloyd and Colin Speke were the duty firemen while teams led by Transport Foreman Jack Howie and Canteen Manager Sid Smith also provided vital services.

Fifty miles away, Radio/Radar Technician Mike Still and his crew were on duty at Mynedd Rhiw, on the Lleyn Peninsula, the lonely outpost overlooking the Range, with a microwave link enabling the Llanbedr transmitter system to cover the Range.

During 1971 Vic Court became a Technical Assistant in the Engineering Development Section. When offered the chance to fly as a Flight Test Observer/Navigator in Llanbedr aircraft, Vic accepted and went on to fly in the Canberra, Meteor, Sea Vixen, Devon and Hawk.

Development trials of the Stiletto supersonic target were completed. Air-launched from the Canberra PR.3, this expendable UK development of the AQM-37A Stiletto supersonic target came into regular use for surface-to-air and air-to-air firings. With its powerful rocket motor and high manoeuvrability, Stiletto's performance envelope included Mach 2.2 up to 70,000 feet, supersonic speed down to 2,000 feet and a maximum speed of

A Beech AQM-37C Stiletto supersonic target drone beneath the starboard wing of Canberra B.2(TT) WH734.

George Hobbs checks a supersonic 'hybrid target' on WH734 prior to take-off.

Mach 3. At Llanbedr the transponders and required flight profile were set and after launching from under the wing of the Canberra, Aberporth took control of the Stiletto.

Meteor U.16 WK800 (ex-RAAF U.21 A77-876) had originally been built as an F.8 by Armstrong Whitworth at Coventry and shipped to Australia in 1955. After conversion by Flight Refuelling Ltd from U.21 to U.16 standard, the aircraft was delivered to RAE Llanbedr in July 1971 and went on to become the only Meteor still operating at Llanbedr after the millennium.

Charlie Harris' obituary list for 1971 included Deputy Chief Storekeeper Charles Staff from Llanfrothen who died at Broadgreen, Liverpool, and Pratts Estate Workers Foreman Gwilyn Owen Davies from Dolgellau.

1972

'Lunch hour shake-up' and 'we witness two lovely pink and white parachutes coming down. Martin-Baker ejection seats had saved two more lives' was how Charlie Harris recorded the crash of a No.4 Flying Training School Folland Gnat T.1 trainer (XR948) from RAF Valley on the edge of the airfield on 14th March. John O'Neill recalled that 'it suffered

The lonely outpost and transmitter at Mynedd Rhiw, on the Lleyn Peninsula.

an engine fire and descended vertically at high power and "tent-pegged" just outside the south-eastern boundary of the airfield.'

Before he handed his OC Flying hat on to Squadron Leader Don E Betts, John had opened the airfield at weekends for special requirements. He recalled: 'I once escorted the great Clough Williams Ellis (Architect of Porthmeirion) and his wife, in their ancient and battered Austin 7 to the Aircraft Servicing Platform where awaited an executive jet, around which were clustered a number of people, mostly politicians of great note at the time. There were Jeremy Thorpe, Lord Byers, Lord Carrington, Lord Callaghan and the Archbishop of Canterbury – Lord Fisher. They were all merrily knocking back champagne. They were off to the West Country to dedicate a memorial designed by Clough Williams Ellis to Mrs Jeremy Thorpe, who had been killed in a tragic road accident.

'When they returned later that afternoon the Ellises were poured out of the aircraft which then took off into the wild blue yonder. Then the great man turned to me and said: "You must call it back. This is not my suitcase!" He had one full of religious vestments! The aircraft was no longer on frequency and the quaint pair finally went home in their ancient jalopy, albeit in enormous grump. I envisioned the next day's headlines – CLOUGH in a HUFF!'

John was helpful to the Lord Lieutenant of Merioneth, Colonel Williams Wynne, who farmed near Towyn. When John was invited to attend a cocktail party at Ty Croes army camp the colonel, who operated his own two-seater light aircraft, arranged to collect John in the aircraft. As John noted: 'Ty Croes did not have a landing strip and the gallant colonel, to the amazement of the watching guests, landed on the football pitch in front of the Officers' Mess. To my horror he nearly took the wheels off on the goal posts at one end and narrowly avoided an own goal at the other! On the return journey I was much relieved that he took my professional advice to take off diagonally across the pitch – after removing the corner flag!'

In May Meteor U.16 WK800 went to RAE West Freugh for 15 months. By the end of September the number of Llanbedr staff with the surname 'Jones' had fallen from 40 to 39 while those named 'Hunter' increased from three to four. This was because aircraft engineer Michael Hunter married Wendy Jones of the Wages office!

From serviceable parts salvaged from damaged Jindiviks and items becoming obsolete with the phasing out of the Mark 103A aircraft, Llanbedr's resourceful engineers 'home-built' an additional Jindivik Mk 103A, 'Llanbedr One', which first flew on 4th October. The 'do-it-yourself' Jindivik brought congratulations from the Director of RAE Farnborough, who said: 'Your staff have demonstrated a high degree of skill and initiative in their endeavour, and have not only saved a lot of public money but also introduced one more target aircraft into the Llanbedr operational fleet which has recently been depleted to an uncomfortably low level.' 'Llanbedr One' went on to earn its keep until brought down by a Sparrow air-to-air missile 15 months later while flying on its 38th sortie.

At this stage in Llanbedr's history 245 pilotless sorties had been flown by 24 Firefly U.8s and 46 Firefly U.9s. Meteor pilotless sorties

The 'home-built' Jindivik, 'Llanbedr One'.

totalled 734. More than 2,600 Jindivik sorties had been flown with 15 Jindivik Mk 102s, 50 Mk 102Bs, 65 Mk 103As and 50 Mk 103Bs having been produced for Llanbedr. In Australia, two prototype Jindiviks were being tested at Woomera with a view to producing a Bell Aerospace Air Cushion Landing System (ACLS) for which the Weapons Research Establishment was collaborating with the United States Air Force. Although useful information was gained the ACLS was not incorporated into production aircraft.

When a young Barmouth girl, Caroline Nash, needed treatment in the United States, Shorts staff at Llanbedr, headed by Charlie Meadows, began fund-raising. The Airfield Social Club committee arranged a benefit dance, Miss Menna Jones (PBX) and Miss Ann Eirwin Jones (Publications) organised a whist drive and further donations raised the target of £650 in time for Caroline and her mother to make the journey in the New Year.

Charlie Harris' obituary list for the year included Cleaner W R Thomas from Harlech and Driver Elwyn Pugh Jones who died in Bangor after a heart attack.

1973

Ministry of Defence project engineers were looking around for suitable aircraft to convert into full-scale drone targets to meet the needs of sponsors. As Basil Jerram noted: 'They envisaged a package in which a unit incorporating all the autopilot, radio, telemetry and control systems could be fitted to the standard ejection seat mountings in any aircraft.' Because the Royal Navy was retiring its carrier-based de Havilland Sea Vixen FAW.2 all-weather interceptors, ten of these twin-boomed aircraft were allocated to the project. Flight Refuelling Ltd was to refurbish selected airframes, incorporate the remote control target system and develop it for operational use.

Two Sea Vixen FAW.2s were allocated to Llanbedr for pilots and engineers to familiarise themselves with the type. New heavy-duty arrester gear was installed to cater for these heavier aircraft. In June the first Sea Vixen arrived in the form of XP924, started in 1963 as an FAW.1 but completed in 1967 as

an FAW.2. The Sea Vixens at Llanbedr were to be used for shepherding, tracking trials, pilot continuation flying and perhaps for the Rushton Tow.

Meteor U.16 WK800 arrived back at Llanbedr in August and RAE West Freugh borrowed the Llanbedr Hunter for some trials. The Hunter's first tasking at Llanbedr had been as a high-speed low-level chase aircraft for Jindivik development trials, but it proved useful in other roles including the capability to put out smoke from canisters.

In November, after seven years 'down under', Gwyn 'Harlech' Jones returned to North Wales and found Llanbedr airfield still shrouded in misty rain! Among his 'firsts' in Australia were becoming the first civilian Strip Engineer to launch from Woomera, the first Strip Engineer to launch from Jervis Bay and the first Team Leader to launch a supersonic missile (Petrel) from Woomera. He found RAE Llanbedr much improved. The new Control Tower had replaced the small wartime building and was equipped with Decca ASR1 radar (80 miles and 60,000 feet), Ground Controlled Approach and a Computed Antenna Direction Finder.

The main runway across the peninsula provided for minimum flight over land by pilotless aircraft. Llanbedr was concentrating on developing Jindivik's potential and although a few Meteors were operating pilotless and piloted sorties the pilotless target sorties were almost always flown by Jindivik with the loss rate brought down to two per cent. Current developments concerned radio-altimeter coupling, with the autopilot being automatically controlled by radio-altimeter sensing to permit an ultra low-level high-speed capability.

'It's arrived!' announced the first issue of the Llanbedr airfield newspaper, edited by J Rhodes. The leaflet had question marks in place of a title. Readers were invited to suggest printable and practicable names for it. The journal reported that 'Charlie' Brown was retiring after eight years with Shorts. Jim Gray was also retiring (to Scotland) after ten years in the Drone Instruments Section. Alun Jones of the Jindivik Hangar was looking for a new car with the assistance of Ken Griffiths. Joyce had presented husband Maurice

Giffin (Radio Section) with a son. Also 'in the news' were Ron Telfer of the Stiletto Section and Dick James of Drone Instruments, both back at work following hospital operations and Canteen Manager Mr Sid Smith for the sharpness of his food slicer! Tommy Green of the Meteor Hangar made the front page for stating that he had reached a turning point in his life. There was no explanation of the last two items! The activities of the RAE Llanbedr Recreational and Social Club filled the last page: cheese and wine party, pottery party, whist drives, drama group activities, darts matches, Christmas and New Year's Eve parties.

Charlie Harris' unpublished obituaries for the year included H Allen Smith, an Air Traffic Control Officer (ATCO) who was killed in a road accident, Cook Mrs Nellie Lewis, Controller Bob Hunter, Groundsman Evan Caetani (heart attack) and Dick James from the Instrument Section.

1974

The second issue of '? ? ?' reported that Chief Aircraft Engineer, Mr D Rossell had left Porthmadoc Hospital to convalesce and that Keith Unwin required a starter motor for his Austin 1100. A photograph of 'Raving beauties Michelle Hunter and Mamie Jones, seen at the Hallowe'en Ball, accompanied by Fairy Godmother Cath Brown' made the front page, not page 3! Arthur Pearcy reminded readers that Jindivik Mk 2 A92-68, in retirement in the Bellman hangar, had done two flights 'down under' at Woomera before being shipped to RAE Farnborough for the 1957 SBAC Show. Arthur also explained that A92-999 was fictitious, a showpiece 'Jindivik' whose motifs of the Welsh dragon and the 'Phoenix sortie symbol' had intrigued the general public when exhibited at shows.

When the MoD reduced the required number of target controllers from eight to six, Short Brothers and Harland Ltd dismissed Graham Biswell and Alan Scott of Harlech on the principle of 'last in, first out'. An industrial tribunal found Mr Scott's dismissal was not unfair, but Mr Biswell was awarded compensation for unfair dismissal because the company had misinterpreted the procedure on redundancies. Later, Graham returned to work at the airfield for many more years.

The February issue of the news leaflet recorded that 'Llanbedr One' 'decided to leave us last month in a blaze of glory.' Arthur Guest, John Hughes, Mick Doyle and Keith Unwin were thanked for their winning apt suggestion of 'TARGET' for the title. Runner-up from the 23 entries was 'AVGAS'! 'TARGET' reported the wedding of Terry Parry to Minette Wannop and that Mrs Margaret Hobbs had made the bride's long dress of mid-blue velvet trimmed with white fur. Mrs Pauline Fairfax-Rawlings was welcomed back to become shorthand typist to the Officer-in-Charge. Club ties were selling well with an order from Woomera for three dozen – and also because of the ruling that MPC pilots who shot down a Jindivik MUST buy one!

On 26th March Chief Aircraft Engineer Dennis Rossell died at the age of 54. According to Wing Commander A R 'Tommy' Atkins: 'Ross was feared, respected and admired. His aircraft were the shiniest to be seen, raising many an admiring glance. There were also shining interiors – a point completely missed by one civil servant who criticised us for bothering to keep them so clean.'

Ross had figured prominently in all the changes that took place from the early 1950s. When he became ill there was no cure and he was taken to Madoc Memorial Hospital where he had a room overlooking the bay towards the airfield. 'He still tried to work from his bed,' recalled Wing Commander Atkins, 'and Jonah (Mr W Jones, who eventually succeeded Ross) and I were very careful or Ross would pick us up. One night he produced his list of tradesmen worthy of promotion. He was thinking years ahead and I seldom departed from this list afterwards.'

Ross asked for progress reports on the Sea Vixens that were to be droned and after the first was air-tested Bob Gaskell and 'Bing' Crosby visited Ross. They sat by his hospital window remarking on the wonderful view – and working out the direction and height of the flypast they performed for Ross on the following day! 'That day was one of his happiest. Ross died a satisfied man,' Wing Commander Atkins asserted and the April issue of

Meteor U.16 WK800 joins fellow Meteor U.16 WA991 in the fleet at Llanbedr. Visible in the background is a Devon C.2 transport.

Target also paid tribute: 'His work at Llanbedr brought Ross into contact with many aspects of the aircraft industry through which he gained many friends. He was especially respected in places such as Tarrant Rushton, Farnborough, Boscombe Down and Aberporth.'

In May George Hobbs became Chief Instrument Engineer/Histogram operator with responsibility for Flight and Drone Instruments, AMPOR, Winch and target systems, the Photographic Section and Supersonic Targets. During the year he visited Australia regarding the purchase of Jindivik Mk 103Bs.

In October HRH the Duke of Edinburgh piloted a Westland Wessex HCC.4 helicopter to Llanbedr to present the Engineering Employers Federation three-star Safe Working Award to Shorts at Llanbedr for its safety record during 1973. The three-year national average injury rate was 41.4 per 1,000 and Llanbedr had achieved 5.1 per 1,000 employees. Prince Philip was accompanied by the Lord Lieutenant of Merioneth, Colonel Williams-Wynne. Long-serving staff Miss J Coward, Mr N A Collings, Mr W A Howie and Mr T G Trenholme were presented to Prince

Philip by the Ministry of Defence man-in-charge of the airfield, Bert Stanley. In marginal weather conditions the Duke watched a Jindivik operation before departing at the controls of a Hawker Siddeley Andover CC.2 of the Queen's Flight.

Also in October, 'Griff the Barber' and his wife Sarah retired simultaneously, the former from his cleaner and tea-maker duties and Sarah after ten years as Canteen Assistant.

Rob Nash reported that Jindivik Mk 3A WRE-418 was destroyed by a missile on 11th October in Australia while on its 285th flight. In time the number of sorties accumulated would earn this particular Jindivik the record for the greatest number of flights by a single Jindivik until 1987.

Back at Llanbedr, Meteor U.16 WK800 began a second tour as a pilotless target on Aberporth Range, and survived for 18 months during which time four stablemates (WF711, VZ508, WK941 and WA991) were shot down or destroyed.

1975

RAE Llanbedr was almost civilianised but for OC Flying, Squadron Leader Don E Betts and his deputy, Flight Lieutenant W Geveaux. Later in the year Don Betts gave up his position, but not before he flew Canberra PR.3 WE146 on its last operational sortie, shepherding Jindivik A92-612 on 3rd February. In the Canberra were 15,000 commemorative covers celebrating the anniversary of the first pilotless target drone sortie at Llanbedr 21 years previously to the day.

There was an unusual level of anxiety on 11th February when 1,600 'special' covers were packed in waterproof containers and fitted into Jindivik A92-610 for the 3,000th sortie by UK Jindiviks. This sortie involved the firing of a BAC Sea Wolf Research and Development missile by a Phantom FGR.2s of 41 Squadron and if the Jindivik was downed the covers would have to be recovered from the sea. Fortunately the Jindivik survived and the covers returned safely to be certified, signed and hand-stamped No.1490 of the BFPS.

After 22 years a freakish accident was repeated on 21st March at Jervis Bay when Jindivik WRE-529 became airborne for its sixth flight with the trolley still attached to the aircraft. This time the trolley was only held to the aircraft by the front suspension arm and various manoeuvres were performed to dislodge it, without success. Then the crew attempted to touch down the combination onto flat ground near the runway in the hope that the front trolley arm might rotate and free the Jindivik. This was unsuccessful and the aircraft and trolley were both written off in spectacular manner. The trolley involved had made no less than 419 take-off runs during its nine years of service.

In Australia the European Launcher Development Organisation moved from Woomera to South America and, as Gwyn Jones noted, scrap merchants were invited to tender for the leftover equipment: 'Two partners in an Adelaide firm of scrap dealers won the contract and were instructed to attend the Da Costa Building. Realising there was to be a Security Clearance, one of them hastily left the room. It was Ronald Biggs and the State Police were only hours behind him.'

When the UK/Australian Joint Projects at Woomera came to an end, 163 aircraft had been used including the two Pikas. Excluding Pika, 2,129 sorties had been flown during which 105 aircraft were lost through malfunctions and 52 as a result of missile strikes. The possibilities and potential of Jindivik continued to be explored, however. After competitive evaluation by the United States Air Force, Jindivik was chosen to examine the feasibility of an air cushion landing and take-off system for remotely piloted vehicles (RPVs). The Royal Australian Navy made available one of its Jindiviks to be modified at GAF in Melbourne. Studies in the USA were indicating that the air cushion landing and take-off concept – similar to the hovercraft – might eventually supplement or even replace the conventional aircraft wheeled undercarriage in some military and civil applications. Depending upon the outcome of ground and wind tunnel tests, actual take-off and landing trials would be completed in early 1976, it was suggested.

At Llanbedr George Hobbs improved the Jindivik take-off trolley once more and Charlie Harris recorded the death from suicide of Miss Rhona Jones from the Accounts Section during the year.

1976

Basil Jerram C.Eng. MIMechE was promoted to Officer-in-Charge of RAE Llanbedr after acting in the position for some months: 'Over the years I saw Government Ministry giving technical and scientific support to the services,' recalled Basil. 'Some branches of the industry were known as the Ministry of Supply, then of Science and Technology and finally the Ministry of Defence (Procurement Executive). The Air Ministry, the Admiralty and the War Office became MoD (Air), MoD (Navy) and MoD (Army). Many Research and Development establishments also survived within the Procurement Executive. RAE Farnborough was one of the largest and best known of these.

'Among Farnborough's many departments such as Aerodynamics, Structures, Chemistry and Mathematics was the Instrument and Trials Department. Within this was

Ranges Division and Superintendent Ranges was responsible for ranges and weapons trials at Larkhill, West Freugh and Cardigan Bay. RAE Aberporth was the Headquarters establishment for Ranges Division with the main radars, cameras and trials instrumentation. The overall planning of weapons trials and liaison with service and civilian customers was under the authority of Aberporth and the Superintendent Ranges. For this reason there were office and residential facilities for service and contractor's personnel and a small airfield for communications flights at Aberporth.

'As Officer-in-Charge at RAE Llanbedr I became responsible to Superintendent Ranges for the provision of the airborne target service, for day-to-day performance and for forward development and improvements to meet current and future project requirements. I had the support of the civilian contractor at Llanbedr, of other contractors with design authority for airframe and systems and of HQ Ministry departments for aspects (including financial) of forward planning and procurement. I had a small number of RAE scientific personnel as project officers for airframe, system and radio developments.

'Jindivik had been conceived as a short-life target aircraft but the potential life of its Viper turbojet far exceeded the life expectancy of the aircraft which was subject to weapons firings and accidents. It became worthwhile to develop decoys to protect the aircraft from destruction but still to provide a realistic aiming point for guided weapons. This was achieved by aerodynamic bodies, stowed on winches under the wings of the Jindivik. During the trial they were deployed some 50 feet or 100 feet behind the aircraft on cables and carrying infra-red or visual flares which were fired at the key moment by remote control. Later on, active and passive radar decoys were developed.

'Because of the permutations of wing, tow, flare, camera and enhancement that might be called up at short notice the daily task of target servicing and preparation became increasingly time-consuming and difficult to manage. This sometimes led to recriminations between those who specified (and sometimes changed) their operational requirements and those who were striving to meet them on time! So it became policy to prepare a fleet of aircraft in most, if not all of the possible configurations on a daily basis. This placed a serious burden on aircraft stocks, on manpower and other resources.

'By studying and redesigning critical interfaces we arrived at a system in which the various winch and tow assemblies were prepared and stored ready for fitting at short notice. Then the extra-high altitude configuration was discontinued as a result of falling operational requirements for it. Thus it became possible to meet the Range's daily operational requirements in a much reduced time scale.

'With the success of the decoy system, deliberate destruction of the aircraft was allowed only when it was an essential element of a weapons trial. In all other cases the final clearance to fire was given only when correct operation of the decoy system was confirmed. In air-to-air firings this was usually by the pilot's visual observation. Telemetered information could also provide the information but these two sources were not always in agreement!

'There were failures that led to aborted trials – the tow release might fail, the tow was sometimes lost if the cable failed, the flares might fail to ignite. Such events were embarrassing when I had to explain to Superintendent Ranges and my Aberporth colleagues, who had to answer to trials sponsors in their turn. So there was always a continued effort to improve reliability and performance.

'New weapons developments called for targets that could fly fast and low, the aim being 500 knots at 50 feet. Under a local initiative a radio-altimeter was integrated into the height control/height lock system and trials demonstrated that the aircraft could be flown down to the required minimum altitude. BAe and Marconi Elliots were then called in to update the airframe and autopilot respectively to provide an operational capability of 500 knots at 50 feet for sponsors. Other developments to improve and update continued in many areas, in line with the latest technology.'

During the year, Charlie Meadows emigrated to the USA and Ken Jones from the

Accumulator Room was killed on the road by The Wayside. In Operations, 'Pete' E F Pennie (ex-RAF officer, Grade 2, Ret'd) was Deputy OC Flying (Unmanned Operations) at RAE Llanbedr with Eric Ainsworth, Bob Gaskell and Peter Shaw as staff pilots.

1977

Llanbedr's Jindivik Mk 103B was a highly successful target aircraft but it was also quite expensive, so the Ministry of Defence (Procurement Executive) began to appraise the Beech MQM-107 jet-powered, zero-launch parachute-recovered system as an eventual replacement. This prompted the Australian Government Aircraft Factories to reduce costs with the Jindivik Mk 4. At the same time Marconi was designing a Universal Drone Pack (UDP) to fit into the ejector seat space of most service aircraft (in particular for the Sea Vixen). The Jindivik Mk 4's electronics were therefore designed to use the UDP, but there were technical difficulties.

After further modification work the Jindivik Mk 4 was fitted with its own Flight Control Computer. The structure was strengthened to increase the g limit to +6. Improved electronics released space for more fuel and a generator replaced the alternator. Further improvements were envisaged and it was agreed that the Anglo-Australian Jindivik Mk 4 Development Project would finance the provision of two prototypes.

Reviewing Jindivik in August, after 234 Jindiviks had been delivered to Llanbedr, the record showed 51 lost through malfunction and 31 to missile strikes. A total of 3,245 sorties had been flown. On the subject of Jindivik loss rate, Ian Fleming pointed out that only ten sorties per aircraft had been expected in the early days. However, the malfunction loss rate at Woomera averaged 1 in 10 over the eight years to 1960, then fell to 1 in 50 from 1961 to 1970 and to 1 in 85 over the next seven years.

Celebrating the Jindivik's Australian Silver Jubilee, Ken Sayers and Noel Jenkinson from Government Aircraft Factories visited Llanbedr, bringing with them copies of their special philatelic cover with the special Jindivik postmark used at Nowra. The anniversary flight carrying the covers was at the Jervis Bay Range Facility where the Shorts civilian flight crew included Ray Gough, a pilot who had worked at Llanbedr before transferring to Australia.

The existence of Llanbedr airfield was welcome, once again, for an aircraft in distress on 19th September after the engine of a Folland Gnat T.1 trainer from RAF Valley flamed out. Squadron Leader Roy Gamblin, OC Standards Squadron, was checking out an instructor who was practising line astern formation on another Gnat T.1. The engine would not relight and Roy transmitted a Mayday call. Llanbedr airfield had just closed for the weekend when staff heard the call and re-opened for the emergency. Roy Gamblin described what happened next:

'We were about eight miles west of Llanbedr but it was covered in cloud with high ground just to the east. Valley, with Mona as back-up, was familiar and had services used to handling our kind of problem. However, our glide capability to reach Valley was tight and there was an 18-knot crosswind. Llanbedr ATC reported their cloud base as 3,500 feet and I decided to dive through the cloud for speed to manoeuvre and take it visually if possible. My lead aircraft was shadowing me and gave us a quick heading correction. We were still IMC at 3,000 feet and I began to consider ejection as we were short of height for a forced landing pattern, in manual, on standby instruments with the gear still up.'

However, his subsequent Green Endorsement concluded: '…he broke cloud at 2,800 feet three miles south-west of the airfield and, by skilful manoeuvring, positioned himself for an approach to the most convenient runway. Lack of hydraulic pressure meant that the flying controls were in manual and thus heavy to handle and, to add to his difficulty, the emergency lowering system failed to lock the undercarriage down until 500 feet on the final approach to land. Nevertheless, Squadron Leader Gamblin made a copybook touchdown at 165 knots, and although the brake parachute failed to stream, brought the aircraft to a standstill 600 feet from the end of the runway. There was no barrier. For his calm handling of a very haz-

ardous situation, together with his display of flying skill and airmanship of a very high order which resulted in the saving of a valuable aircraft, Squadron Leader Gamblin is awarded a Green Endorsement.'

During 1977 Chief Pilot Eric Ainsworth was presented with the Jubilee Medal and Fireman Meirion W Jones received a special award for his exceptional performance at the Air Force Department Fire School. In November ex-RAF pilot Len Morgan joined the Operations staff: 'But I didn't fly for a month as there was an industrial dispute going on because Eric Ainsworth and Bob Gaskell didn't want to retire from flying at 55 years!'

According to Charlie Harris, deaths during the year were those of Accounts Clerk R W Williams and the Battery Room's Gwilym Jones of Salem.

1978

With the dispute resolved, Len began flying. Already familiar with the Meteor, Gnat and Hunter aircraft at Llanbedr, he went on to convert onto the Devon C.2, Canberra B.2(TT), Sea Vixen D.3 and Hawk T.1.

Another 21st anniversary was that of the first Meteor drone target on 29th January for which souvenir covers were prepared. The 'Vintage Nugget' formation comprised Meteor T.7 WA662 (Squadron Leader M V Doherty, OC Flying), Meteor U.16 WK800 (Eric Ainsworth, Chief Pilot), Meteor U.16 WH320 (Bob Gaskell) and Meteor NF.11 WD790 (Bruce S Bull with Vic Court on board as photographer). On 26th January the formation flew to Aberporth Range Head and returned, after which the covers were certificated and distributed.

The introduction of an age limit for pilots of single-seat jet aircraft made the 'Vintage Four' unique in terms of the age of the aircraft and the pilots so they flew once more with a fifth Meteor (WH453) to photograph the historic formation. Unfortunately a fuel tankers' dispute held up the mission until 19th May, by which time the ages of the five Meteors totalled 132 years and 10 months and the ages of the five pilots (Eric Ainsworth, Bob Gaskell, Peter Shaw, Tommy Thomson and Bruce Bull) totalled 272 years with 33,163 flying hours between them! Bruce Bull became known as the 'Canberra King'

Above: **This Gnat T.1 from 4 FTS at RAF Valley ran off the runway at Llanbedr after a forced landing by Squadron Leader Roy Gamblin (inset).** Both Roy Gamblin collection

Opposite page, top: **Eric Ainsworth and Bob Gaskell 'didn't want to retire from flying'.**

Centre: **The second 'Vintage Nugget' formation of Meteor U.16s WK800/Z, WH453/L and WH320/W and Meteor T.7 WA662.**

Bottom: **Peter Pennie retires in style aboard Jindivik A92-415.**

having accumulated more flying hours on the type than anyone else in the world, according to Vic Court. Eric and then Bob retired from jet-flying in accordance with the age limit introduced by the Director of Flying MoD(PE), but continued to fly Llanbedr's piston-engined Devon C.2 for several years.

In July George Hobbs became New Projects Engineer with a programme including the introduction of the Sea Vixen D.3, the Jindivik Mk 4A and the Rushton Mk 3 towed target system. The first Llanbedr flight trials of the Rushton Mk 3 took place in August. Canberra B.2 WE121 was crewed by Peter Shaw (pilot) and Vic Court. Basil Jerram described the Mk 3: 'The Rushton system presented a cylindrical body, suitably enhanced, on a very long cable (up to 23,00 feet) to permit missile firings against the target with no risk to the parent aircraft. The target was deployed and recovered by means of a winch driven by an air turbine. For maximum operational flexibility the Rushton target was carried on one wing and Stiletto on the other.'

Charlie Harris recorded that heart attacks caused the deaths of Radio technician Bill Williams, Clerk of Works Tommy Thomas, past Officer-in-Charge Bert Stanley and Administrator Frank Dobney. Also Jeff Trenholme from the Electrical Section died following prolonged illness.

1979

During the year the Decca ASR1 radar, which had given good service, according to Derek Whitehead, was replaced by a Plessey AR15/2B and the original PAR was replaced by a modified ex-service Model 3B. In July George Hobbs returned to Australia in connection with the Jindivik Mk 4A 800 series and the news broke that the tender submitted to the Ministry of Defence by Short Brothers for renewal of their contract for five years from October had not been accepted. Manager Mr John Rhodes told the press that his company had held the Llanbedr contract since 1951. There were reassurances that most jobs should be safe, however.

Basil Jerram recalled: 'Despite all the compelling arguments put forward to defend the status quo, Government policy had forced Contracts Branch to seek competitive tender for the renewal of the service and operating contract at Llanbedr. Morale at Llanbedr, Farnborough and other establishments was falling steadily. When the long-established contractors, Short Brothers and Harland, lost the competition, with them went some much-valued members of staff.'

The Llanbedr contract went to Airwork Services Ltd at Bournemouth-Hurn Airport, who re-appointed George Hobbs as Chief Technical Officer, responsible for all engineering aspects at RAE as well as continuing as New Projects Engineer. However, within a few weeks George became Technical Manager. Charlie Meadows was drawn back to Llanbedr as a leading hand, eventually to become Chief Engineer (Mechanical) ten years on, when Ralph Highley retired. But Charlie's first week back at Llanbedr was interrupted by a dreadful accident.

Disaster struck when Canberra B.2(TT) WH734 was under maintenance in the Manned Aircraft Hangar on 11th October. Working in the cockpit of a Meteor alongside, Charlie Meadows heard the initial bang and knew that a Canberra ejection seat had fired. After the clatter of debris settled he saw the hole in the hangar roof and jumped down from the Meteor. He saw Armament Fitter Trevor Caldwell fall out of the Canberra, missing one arm. While Charlie secured his tie around the stump, Dennis Westley climbed up to the roof to fetch Trevor's arm, hoping the surgeons could save it. Unfortunately this wasn't possible. The cause of the accident was using the incorrect size of spanner for disarming the ejection seat. The spanner had therefore slipped onto the wrong part of the sequence, firing the seat without severing the controls. 'That really aged me!' said Charlie.

Since 1960 Jindiviks had gradually taken over the task of providing a drone target service on Aberporth Range; consequently the number of pilotless Meteor sorties declined. In 1979 there was just one Meteor sortie, resulting in the shootdown of U.16 WH320.

Charlie Harris wound up his faithful record with the report that Robin 'Canteen' Roberts and Leslie Scott, an ATCO, suffered fatal heart attacks during the year.

Airwork Services Ltd appoint George Hobbs (on steps, wearing tie) to be Technical Manager.

The aftermath of the accidental firing of Canberra B.2(TT) WH734's pilot ejection seat during maintenance.

Standing: Derek Whitehead (Radio/Electronic Development); Robin Harper, MoD (Target Development); Phil Williams (Radio/Electronic Development); John Lees, MoD (Target Development); Hedley Whitfield, MoD (Radio/Electronic Development); Chief Security Officer; Ted Short, MoD (Admin Officer); Mike Balderstone (Target Development); Seated: Sandra Williams (Office Assistant); Basil Jerram (Officer-in-Charge); Irene Roberts (Secretary to Officer-in-Charge).

ATC Assistant Audrey Pearcy (with flowers) on the day of her retirement.

Chapter Six

The 1980s

1980

There were no pilotless Meteor sorties in 1980, but Meteors continued to serve as shepherd aircraft, for target controller training and testing equipment and procedures. Two Jindiviks were shot down and another broke up during a development flight. The Ministry of Defence ordered 40 production Jindivik Mk 4s, but then reduced the order to 15 to make savings.

1981

In a busy year for the Canberras with a variety of towed targets, Winch Operator Vic Court's most rewarding time was during RAF Exercise 'Granulla' on the Royal Artillery Range Hebrides, launching Stiletto targets on five long sorties. Vic remembered the work involved in the exercise: 'We flew each sor-

tie from Llanbedr so we had a 45-minute transit flight to and from the Hebrides, leaving us about two hours on task. Pre-flight preparation involved reading and digesting the Op Order for launch position, altitude, speed, heading, callsigns, and r/t frequencies. I had to look up the Met to plan each flight taking winds and temperatures into account so as to estimate flight times, fuel consumption and reserves. Suitable diversion airfields had to be selected for possible problems at the various stages of the sortie.

Viewed through the canopy of a Hawk T.1, Canberra B.2(TT) WH734 is seen carrying a Rushton target (port) and an AQM-37C Stiletto supersonic target (starboard). Note the high-visibility black and yellow diagonal banding on the undersides, to signify the aircraft's use in the target-towing role.
Vic Court collection

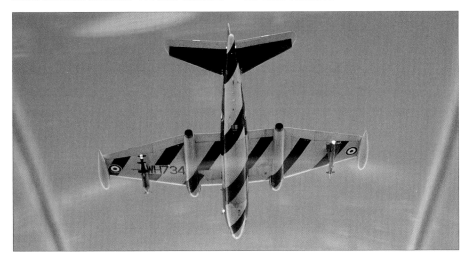

Jindivik A92-664 reaches a century of sorties on 10th July 1981.

Marking the 4,000th Jindivik sortie from Llanbedr on 22nd December 1981.

'During the sortie I helped with navigation and looked after the Stiletto because during transit various target checks had to be carried out. On range I had to run up the Stiletto and after a countdown operate the launch switch.

'I did my first Stiletto launch with pilot Flight Lieutenant Tommy Thompson and went on to do four more flying with other pilots. The first time is quite nerve-racking because you know the Stiletto is a dangerous beast if it were to misbehave. It felt good after the target was launched and we flew home knowing we had presented a good target. I have had one that failed to launch and we carried out various pre-planned procedures to try and get rid of it, but when these failed we just had to make it safe and return to base.'

In April Lord Strathcona's Working Group recommended further devolution of project-orientated work to industry and recommended contractorising domestic and support services and facilities, including Ranges – and therefore Llanbedr. In Australia the first prototype Jindivik Mk 4 was delivered to Jervis Bay as N11-800 for flight-testing which

was completed in July; it was expected that N11-802 would be ready the following year.

At Llanbedr three of the year's four drone Meteor sorties flown were undertaken by WK800. The fourth, on 8th December, was the last for seven years. From 782 sorties since July 1958, 121 drone Meteors were shot down, written off or destroyed. Jindivik achievements during 1981 included A92-664 being the first UK Jindivik to reach 100 flights on 10th July and A92-716 making the 4,000th UK Jindivik flight on 12th December.

1982

When BAe Hawk T.1 XX154 arrived from Dunsfold on 18th January, to be a Jindivik Shepherd and Trials Aircraft, followed by Hawk T.1s XX160 and XX170, Hangar Foreman Gary Jones welcomed them: 'When the MoD called for an advanced trainer in 1970, Hawker Siddeley Aviation presented their low-wing, tandem-seat design and were awarded a contract for 175 machines and a pre-production aircraft (XX154). Five aircraft

Hawk T.1 XX154 takes off from Llanbedr.

would be kept back for the flight development programme – the fifth was XX160. Hawk XX154 was built on production jigs and was probably the first British military aircraft to be produced without benefit of a prototype.

'XX154 arrived here with 406 hours 10 minutes flight time, low on the RAF minimum modification standard, the aircraft still wired up with strain gauges, an inferior avionics system and was probably the only Hawk to have cable-operated brakes. With the arrival of XX170, XX154 went to RAF Abingdon and returned a much-improved machine.'

XX154 saw out the 20th century at Llanbedr before its duties were passed to the Dornier Alpha Jet, but sadly Gary did not survive cancer to see this. Converting to Hawks 'was a most enjoyable task, because the Hawk was perfect, harmonised and too good for students,' said RAF pilot Bill Downs on his first tour at Llanbedr as Deputy to the OC Flying, Squadron Leader 'Tin Leg' Tyldesley. Four years later, Bill became Security and Admin Manager at Llanbedr on retirement from the RAF.

Bob Gaskell was obliged to hang up his leather flying helmet as had Eric Ainsworth. 'I could tell you a few stories about the "fiddles" when it came to yet another year's extension to the flying careers of that magnificent duo. Talk about the Peter Pans of the aviation world!' said Andrew Fyall. Superintendent of Ranges from 1976 to 1987, Andrew often flew to meetings in the Devon ferry aircraft piloted by Eric and Bob. 'There was an air of faded gentility about the aircraft AND the crew! Despite some hair-raising moments I did feel safe with them.' Len Morgan and Steve Ives (ex-RAF navigator) became the next regular ferry 'duo' and the trio (Len, Steve and Devon C.2 XA880) went on to fly over 450 hours together.

During the summer George Hobbs spent several weeks in Australia for the flight trials of the Jindivik Mk 4A 800 series. The second prototype was N11-801; 15 production aircraft for the UK (Mk 4As) were numbered A92-802 to A92-816. Before the end of the year A11-801 achieved 535 knots at 50 feet.

At Llanbedr, Basil Jerram recalled, 'having committed ourselves to achieving high g

manoeuvres – a step into the unknown – the Sparrow development and firing trials were satisfactorily completed to time.' However, during the year the MoD withdrew their Project Officer from RAE Llanbedr and the Engineering Development Section was created. Officer-in-Charge Basil Jerram paid tribute and presented engraved plaques to J Lees, Mr H Whitfield, R Harper and ETN Short on their retirement. He also said farewell to the RAE and the management of Llanbedr was handed to Airwork Services Ltd.

1983

As in previous years several Jindiviks were lost through shootdowns, accidents, technical or controller difficulties over 144 sorties. The Model 3B PAR was replaced by a CR62. In April Meteor U.16 WK800 went to Marshalls of Cambridge to be modified for some trials, leaving U.16 WH453 and T.7 WA662 as the only two remaining Meteors at Llanbedr. In Australia Jindivik A11-801 achieved 535 knots at 410 feet.

1984

This year saw the old control tower refurbished. Removing the traditional balcony, external steps and access to the roof drove the Operations Staff out of the building and into the Canteen for six months. George Hobbs travelled to Australia once more to assist with the final assembly and testing of the first production Jindivik Mk 4A 800 series aircraft (A92-802) at Avalon and also revisited Jervis Bay. John Kendrick had become OC Flying and Ian P Smith arrived to become Engineering Development Officer.

1985

Parked outside the ATC headquarters near the Main Gate at Llanbedr Airfield for years, Anson T.21 VS562 had served the cadets well but was by now unsafe. Acquired by a scrap-merchant equipped with a circular saw to reduce the airframe to sections for road transport, VS562 went away – only to return a few years later!

1986

De Havilland Sea Vixen D.3 XP924 in the high-visibility yellow and red drone livery.

The distinctive swept-back wings and high twin-tail of Sea Vixen D.3 XP924 reappeared in the skies around Llanbedr, the aircraft now resplendent in the highly distinctive red and yellow drone livery. Converted at Tarrant Rushton, XP924 was to be flown with a safety pilot to explore the possibilities of a supersonic drone. Unfortunately various problems were never overcome and this project was eventually abandoned.

Ian Smith became Airwork's Officer-in-Charge and Keith Paine took over as Engineering Development Officer. 'My first project was getting clearance for the Canberra's 30k tow cable with low level height-keeper targets for vertical launch Sea Wolf missiles,' said Keith. 'Then I had to learn about Jindiviks and get involved with the development of AGS. At that time there was no method of recording what buttons were pressed, so on the first flight trial, with Bob and Eric in the Control Cell, flying the Pulse Controlled Modulation Sea Vixen on AGS, I videoed the duplicate control consoles in the AGS Portakabin from above.'

1987

On 7th July I joined the OPS staff to become a Target Controller. John Kendrick, the OC Flying/Operations Manager was welcoming but Eric Ainsworth, Deputy OC Flying Unmanned made clear his disapproval of a female presence, even in the tea bar! He ran the 'tea swindle' (very efficiently) and made it plain that this particular operation was his baby and I would incur much wrath if I so much as switched on the kettle or did the washing up! I enjoyed this 'reverse discrimination' for the short time that it lasted!

My first memory of Bob Gaskell was the gruff reply to a question: "I'm not answering that – I'm not training you to take my job!" (Some hope!) However it wasn't long before he asked me to join his ATC Squadron at Blaenau Ffestiniog as a civilian instructor – so that the squadron could enrol girls! I did so and found the enthusiasm and success of the female cadets very rewarding.

Llanbedr Ops comprised John Kendrick, Len Morgan and Brian Hood (all ex-RAF pilots); Staff Navigator was Steve Ives (ex-RAF) and Target Controller David 'Bomber' Brown (an ex-RN pilot) also sometimes flew as an Observer/Winch Operator, as did Vic Court. In addition to Eric and Bob, the Target Controllers were Peter Shaw (an ex-RAF pilot and son of pioneer airline pilot Captain 'Gerry' Shaw), Dan Carter (an ex-Fleet Air Arm pilot who had flown in the Korean War) and John Adams (an ex-RAF navigator). Manning the Ops Desk overlooking the airfield was Tony Townshend and there was also Snoopy, John Kendrick's amiable on the operational aspects of introducing new target aircraft systems.

On 13th July I 'observed' Azimuth Controller David Brown during a Jindivik sortie. I climbed into the back of the 'Ops Land Rover' and Dave sat in front beside a driver from the Motor Transport section. We towed the Azimuth trailer, painted in large red and white squares, around the airfield to the main runway and positioned it on the extended centreline. We dragged 30-foot cables to the supply point, connected them and switched on. Up in the control cabin were two control desks side by side, each mounted on a pedestal and each with a set of hand controls at waist level. Above each desk were powerful fixed binoculars that could be adjusted and fixed in the vertical plane and panned horizontally through about 160 degrees for tracking the Jindivik on base leg and finals.

On the runway a Jindivik was being prepared by ground crew. Cables and a fuel pipe linked it to the support vehicle alongside while a fire engine also stood by.

Through headphones I heard the voices of Air Traffic, Aberporth, the Shepherd pilot, Master Controller, Skipper, Navigator, Data Room, Strip Engineer and Dave working through the rundown procedures. Eventually the Skipper said: 'Azimuth, Take Control.' There was a squealing noise until Dave pressed his 'Accept Control' button. As the Jindivik accelerated away from us down the runway, Dave steered it using his left/right joystick. When the Jindivik flew off the trolley, Dave pressed his 'STRAIGHT' button and the Jindivik climbed away while the trolley slowed and stopped on the runway. The Skipper reported 'One hundred and ninety knots', the Jindivik pitched up as the flaps came up and Dave beeped it into a right turn.

Then we had to pack up and trundle round the peritrack to the other end of the runway to set up for the landing. We scanned the western horizon through our binoculars until we could see the returning Jindivik, shepherded by a Hawk. 'Turn target right, base leg' and 'Select Straight' then 'three miles to the final turn', and 'Talkdown on target at five miles, stand by right turn final approach', then 'Turn target right now!'

The Azimuth Control trailer lined up for a Jindivik launch.

pooch. I was the replacement for 'Paddy' Dalzell whose career as a target controller had ended six months previously for medical reasons.

John Kendrick wished to draft the Jindivik Mk 4A Manual differently from the cumbersome Mk 3 'bible'. When he found I was happy to help with this on my computer, I was moved from the smoky disapproving ambience of the upstairs crew-room to a desk in the corner of the briefing-room. I enjoyed learning about Jindivik operations from this task and left 'the brethren' (John Kendrick's name for his senior male staff) undisturbed. Later on it was a pleasant surprise to receive a fee of £200 (less tax) for my contribution to the Mk 4A Manual from Contract Manager Ian Smith!

Held in affectionate respect at Llanbedr was Alan Woodcock, an ex-RAF Wing Commander and test pilot from the Instrument and Trials Division at RAE Farnborough. He was responsible to John Knight (head of IT6) for monitoring operations and procedures at RAE Llanbedr and for liaison with the Directorate of Target and Guided Weapons staff

As the Jindivik came out of the finals turn three acquisition lights came into view. After 'Pitch on Target' and 'Az on Target' were called, the Skipper delegated control to them. Dave worked his left/right and straight controls with his hands to keep the Jindivik on the extended centreline. The Skipper read off Jindivik speed and power settings continuously for the Pitch Controller and Air Traffic Control interjected the range to touchdown every half-mile. When the Jindivik landed on its skid, Dave continued to beep left and right as it careered towards us until it came to rest skewed into wind.

Five sorties later I steered the Jindivik during the take-off, approach and landing for the first time. New controllers were supposed to begin training on the Meteor with a safety pilot, but sometimes it wasn't available. When it did appear I found it very different to control from the Jindivik. However, in September I was given 'solo' Meteor sorties and also tried my hand with the Sea Vixen. Equipped for a development flight with the

Sparks fly as a Jindivik makes a night landing at Llanbedr.

forthcoming computerised control system (AGS), and carrying a safety pilot, I was steering the Sea Vixen D.3 down the runway centreline when the airframe disappeared from sight in a cloud of exhaust and dust. I could just see two swirling vortices in the murk and steered those. On lift-off XP924 emerged from the obscuring cloud and I turned her seawards breathing a sigh of relief.

Later that month I observed some operational sorties at night. The Jindivik landing was a pyrotechnic spectacular as it touched down in a blaze of sparks and exhaust that trailed it along the runway, making it difficult for the Azimuth Controller to see the reference lights by which to steer.

One day I joined Ken Griffith's team to observe the groundcrew role during a Jindivik sortie. Ken (related to 'Ma Griff' of wartime café fame) had been a Jindivik Strip Engineer for 20 years and had worked on Meteors when there was a full hangar of them and also on towed targets.

In October eight operational sorties were achieved and November was a mix of operational and training sorties. The Jindivik Mk 4 flew in the UK for the first time and went on to development trials covering high and low

altitudes and rapid manoeuvring. Jindivik A92-810 made its maiden flight and before we stood down for Christmas I qualified as an Azimuth Controller with my first Jindivik solo sortie. By then I was enthralled by Llanbedr's drone operations in which so many people and units collaborated, often with split-second timings, to produce a successful firing sortie, several times a day when required to do so.

Among those units was the Strike Command Air-to-Air Missile Establishment (pronounced 'stackarmi') whose task it was to facilitate the testing and proving of the air-to-air missiles in service with front-line aircraft. Based at RAF Valley on Anglesey, STCAAME had specialised sections for missile telemetry and high-speed photography. RAF Phantom and Lightning air defence fighters were regular users but other NATO aircraft also used this unique service and Panavia Tornado GR.1/F.2, BAe Harrier GR.3, Blackburn Buccaneer S.2B and SEPECAT Jaguar GR.1 aircraft were coming onto the scene as the Phantoms and Lightnings were retired.

BAe Sky Flash and the AIM-9L Sidewinder air-to-air missiles would see out the 20th century but the last Fighter Command Missile Practice Camp firing of a Red Top missile took place from Lightning F.6 XR724 over Cardigan Bay. The new generation of surface-to-air and air-to-air missiles, including the US-produced AIM-120A Advanced Medium Range Air-to-Air Missile (AMRAAM) and the European Advanced Short Range Air-to-Air Missile (ASRAAM) were to follow in the 21st century.

Most of STCAAME's live missile firings took place, courtesy of RAE Llanbedr and RAE Aberporth, in the Cardigan Bay Range, although the larger Royal Artillery Range Hebrides was used for certain high-speed high-level firings. Of the three main missile-firing categories at STCAAME, the No-notice scrambles by QRA and Short-Notice Exercise launches using ready-use missiles were designed to test the readiness and reliability of the whole weapon system: aircraft, crew and missiles. These sorties were usually flown from home base although the aircraft recovered to RAF Valley for debriefing.

For pre-planned Missile Practice Camps a squadron detached several aircraft to STCAAME once a year for several days to fire from four to six missiles on specific attack profiles. These missiles were usually modified to include telemetry transmitters and each firing was analysed closely through films from the firer, Jindivik, a photo-chase

On the runway, observing target rolling.

aircraft, telemetry records, radar-tracking data and miss-distance measurements. A report was produced and the firing classified a success or failure. This enabled fighter tactics or weapon deployment to be proven or amended as indicated. The final benefit was that crews had a rare opportunity to put theory into practice.

Aberporth Range comprised 1,600 square miles of Cardigan Bay, the target area being entirely over water. However, the instrumentation capabilities allowed the tracking and monitoring of trials aircraft well outside this area. The Range specialised in the flight-testing of anti-aircraft and anti-ship guided weapons with facilities at the rangehead for launching missiles, although most were launched from aircraft and ships.

The Range's own workshops produced a comprehensive array of sea targets for anti-ship weaponry while RAE Llanbedr provided the airborne targets. For safety purposes Aberporth operated a computer-based system using 'real-time' tracking radar data to predict the missile debris fallout area associated with the instantaneous position of the missile. Certain missiles were fitted with self-destruct units which could be triggered by ground control should pre-determined safety boundaries be violated.

On request RAE Llanbedr staff prepared, launched and flew, by remote control, a Jindivik target 'dressed' according to a particular specification. On leaving the circuit, Llanbedr ATC handed over the direction of the Jindivik sortie to Range Control at Aberporth. Over the sea the decoy tows were streamed to either 40 feet or 200 feet (the latter distance for a live warhead) and the target flown to the required height. Another Aberporth Range Controller directed the fighters while the Jindivik was headed into a clear area called the 'firing box' for the target 'presentation'. If all went well, we would hear a countdown followed by the calls: 'Firing Now' and 'Stores Away'.

RAE Llanbedr could also provide the Stiletto high-speed target powered by a twin-fuel rocket motor giving a Mach 0.95 performance at low level and Mach 2+ above 50,000 feet. The latter target profile required the use of Royal Artillery Range Hebrides.

Ex-Luftwaffe pilot Sepp Pauli poses for the camera in front of a Meteor U.16 sporting a suitably adorned nose wheel door.

The Stiletto was launched from under the wing of one of RAE Llanbedr's Canberras and climbed or descended to a pre-set target altitude, accelerating to a velocity determined by a pre-set thrust level in the rocket motor. Telemetry provided the miss-distance achieved by the missile firing.

Before the end of the year John Kendrick left to become an airline pilot and ex-Luftwaffe staff pilot Sepp Pauli, was promoted to become OC Flying/Operations Manager. When we closed for Christmas just seven Jindivik sorties were required to reach the landmark figure of 5,000 UK Jindivik sorties, so plans were made to invite all the personnel who had been involved with the first sortie over 28 years ago to a party.

In Australia the record for the greatest number of flights by one Jindivik was broken during the year by N11-530 of the Royal Australian Navy. Rob Nash recorded how N11-530 had been converted to an air cushion landing system for USAF/NASA tests before returning to Royal Australian Navy service and being lost through an equipment failure on the 324th flight.

1988

On 15th January Jindivik A92-733 was launched for a partly operational, partly development sortie which was also the 5,000th UK Jindivik sortie. This achievement was celebrated on 11th February with a party on Shell Island. A smaller dinner party was held a week later at the Castle Cottage Restaurant to mark the retirement of Alan Woodcock. The entertainment included the reading by Alan of a ditty composed by Bethan, and everyone also enjoyed hearing Dave Brown advising Sepp Pauli how to fly a Sea Vixen!

Alan's Llanbedr responsibilities passed to ex-RAF Wing Commander Frank R Guard, who recalled: 'I was a lesser mortal, being an ex-spec 'N' Navigator, RAF. We always maintained that it took a clever fellow to fly on half a wing!'

In late January the Lightnings came on Range for the last time before their retirement from RAF service. They and North American F-100 Super Sabres were considered for 'droning' but the proposal didn't take off. As Frank Guard noted, the result of this decision was that 'the current Meteors and even the Sea Vixen had to be considered for life extensions. The Sea Vixen was put on a limited servicing schedule to keep it in readiness. The Meteors were given fatigue-life extensions and new engines were found in France which enabled the continuance of limited Meteor flying.'

After qualifying on 'Az', life became even more interesting. When a Pitch Controller thumped a Jindivik down a bit too firmly, I seemed to be steering a cloud of dust along the runway! Then an operational Jindivik returned to Llanbedr its tow cable wrapped around the ventral flare-pack. Another new experience was 'Azzing' a Jindivik returning with a tow trailing 40 feet behind. With no rudder the Azimuth Controller operates the ailerons to turn the Jindivik and then selects Straight to neutralise the ailerons and level the wings. In crosswinds 'Az' levels the wings before touchdown and Pitch must avoid floating the Jindivik – for obvious reasons.

My Azimuth experiences soon included landing downwind, with a tow, because of a faulty plug. Another time, with the trailer rocking in the wind, I was peering into grey squalls of rain hoping to see the Jindivik in time to line it up for a landing, and did so, just! In a crosswind it was all too easy to ground-loop the Jindivik on touchdown or to be unable to prevent it drifting into the runway-edge lights (then on stalks) as the speed decayed and control effectiveness faded. On one occasion the trolley nose wheel started shredding up during take-off, too late to abort without damaging the Jindivik, but with separation from the trolley vital before it became unsteerable.

There was the comforting philosophy that Target Controllers weren't qualified until they'd bent a few Jindiviks and the phrase 'it's done some gardening' was the cheerful explanation for a Jindivik ending up on the grass beside the runway. In spite of the recognition that occasional landing damage to remote-controlled aircraft was inevitable and acceptable, lessons were learned and revised techniques, equipment and procedures introduced.

In February my training for Pitch Controller began. In March pilot Brian Hood left and Stan Hodgkins moved to Chalgrove to become Chief Test Pilot with Martin-Baker. Replacements were ex-RAF pilots Andy Carolan and Roy Gamblin. Not for the first time, Chris Merritt, an ex-RAF navigator, joined OPS to be a Target Controller; he had already done a stint in Australia as the 'BATS' controller at Jervis Bay in the 1970s. A Jindivik sortie was laid on to evaluate whether the Hunting Jet Provost was capable of shepherding Jindivik to free up the Hawk T.1s. It wasn't!

During April I did plenty of 'Azzing' on both operational and training sorties with Jindivik and became quite confident with late acquisitions in poor visibility. Also I was training in Pitch on both Meteor and Jindivik. In the middle of the month we started flying the Jindivik Mk 4A. Then on 11th May, A92-802 broke up during a development flight at 2,000 feet at well over 500 knots, apparently due to flutter. Engineering Development Officer Keith Paine said afterwards: 'Darryl Raggott, one of the Aussie sponsors, saw the accelerometer trace start to oscillate and

Hangar staff after the
5,000th Jindivik sortie.

Collecting the trolley after
launching the 5,000th
Jindivik sortie.

The Target Controller crew
after the 5,000th sortie.

directed: "Throttle shut, Skipper!" When I saw over his shoulder that all the telemetry had gone quiet, I uttered an expletive, as we guessed what must have happened. As always, for the investigation, the tape recording from the environmental microphone in the Control Cell was transcribed. It read: Darryl said "throttle shut Skipper" then someone else said "shut". I was amused to see that my expletive (a four-letter word starting with 's' and ending with 't' was transcribed as "shut"!'

I was the Azimuth Controller for Jindivik A92-802's departure and now it wasn't coming back for me to steer it through the landing. Thereafter whenever I was on 'Az' and a Jindivik was lost during the sortie, a sense of unfinished business lingered. Breaching the flutter boundary and the loss of A92-802 brought the Jindivik Mk 4 trials to a halt, but as Frank Guard noted: 'A sound report written by Ian Smith and supported by the Aerospace Technologies of Australia team explained the circumstance and cause of the accident sufficiently to allow further trials and eventually the clearance of the Jindivik Mk 4.'

In May there was a dummy run for 'Twin Jindivik' sorties in which two Jindiviks were presented simultaneously. We rehearsed with one Jindivik and the Sea Vixen. In June two Jindiviks were positioned on the runway. Each had its individual Cell crew, strip crew and frequencies whereas the Pitch and Azimuth Controllers out on the airfield controlled each Jindivik in turn. On 'Az' I did my rundown checks with each Jindivik separately, steered the first Jindivik through the take-off, changed frequencies and steered the second Jindivik take-off ten minutes later.

After moving to the other end of the runway the timing of the Jindiviks returning to the circuit allowed us to land the first Jindivik and the strip crew to clear it from the runway so that we could land the second Jindivik a few minutes later. If either Jindivik could not be recovered safely within its endurance margin, it was to be destroyed. The Master Controller had the challenging task of co-ordinating the whole show. Happily the sortie was a success and both Jindiviks returned safely. Thereafter 'Twin Jindis' became part of our repertoire.

In June Meteor U.16 WK800 returned from Marshall's of Cambridge having been modified for a fourth tour, but between 2nd July and 17th October there was no target flying because the main (target) runway was being resurfaced. Limited manned flying took place from the short runways but the 'down' time was used for servicing and refurbishing all round the airfield. While the Control Tower was refurbished the Air Traffic Controllers shared the OPS room to provide an advisory service. The repartee and banter in Operations trebled during that fortnight! A notice on the Operations board warned:

This side for:	This side for:
OPERATIONS	**AIR TRAFFIC CONTROL**
PLAIN ENGLISH	JARGON & GOBBLEDIGOOK
LOCAL TIME	ZULU TIME

"What does XX154 EX VY mean?" an ATCO asked Tony. "It's shorthand for Hawk XX154 departing from RAF Valley. 'EX' means 'out of' and 'VY' is short for Valley. Simple," he replied. "But RAF Valley's designator is EGOV" objected the ATCO.

During the refurbishment Canberra TT.18 WE121, crewed by Sepp Pauli and Vic Court, was detached on exercise to Gibraltar. Describing one of his least enjoyable flying experiences, Vic told me: 'The Met briefing forecast predicted a very high risk of being struck by lightning and the aircrew manual for the Canberra TT.18 warns "Do not tow targets if there is a high static risk." I suggested to my pilot that we stood a very high chance of being struck by lightning and losing the tow. Nevertheless we took off. We were struck by lightning and lost the tow! There was an extremely loud bang corresponding with a vivid white flash outside all the windows. My towing instruments then showed that we had lost the tow so I advised against streaming the second tow on the grounds that the first winch might be wrecked and we should not go on to wreck the other one.

'A Flight Refuelling Falcon also got struck by lightning and sustained damage to the nose cone. I suspect they only took off because we did and they didn't want to be outdone by Llanbedr! Our winch was damaged, the towing reel had come out and was

'It's done some gardening.' Jindivik A92-708 in a sorry state.

Darryl Raggott (left), Australian sponsor, presenting a Jindivik plaque to George Hobbs.

'Twin Jindiviks' being prepared for take-off on Runway 18.

near to breaking free. It could have fallen off the aircraft at any time.'

In September a programme of refamiliarisation, training and proving new equipment began. There were training sorties with both Jindivik and manned Meteor U.16 WH453. On 24th October Dan Carter was nominated Master Controller for the last Jindivik training sortie before we declared ourselves fully operational once more. All went well during the rundown and take-off. The Jindivik was turned seawards and left the circuit. With little to do until the Jindivik returned, Dan, as was the wont of most Master Controllers of that era, lit a cigarette and leaned back in his chair to savour it. 'Hey, you'll set off the new fire alarms,' warned SATCO Jack Forster just a second too late. The fire alarms sounded and the fire engines promptly responded. Out on the airfield in the control sites we saw the fire engines racing across the airfield and were impressed with the heroism of our colleagues who appeared to be staying at their posts during the fire to bring the Jindivik back for us to land it. But when we returned to the tower there was no sign of smoke or damage, just a slightly sheepish Master Controller!

In November the 'magnificent duo' broke up when Eric Ainsworth retired leaving Bob Gaskell as Deputy OC Unmanned Flying. We dined out Eric and his wife Beryl and along with the usual glassware we presented him with a scroll recalling that '… by skill or mischance Eric flew 5,892 hours in 40 different types of aircraft, thereafter serving countless of the most exquisite and refreshing mugs of tea ever served or yet to be served in Operations … has numbered more than 2,800 sorties with Pilotless Target Aircraft as a Target Controller … has won an endorsement for low flying contrary to Standing Orders … to be sorely missed from the chair behind the crew-room door at lunch times … well-remembered for his words of wisdom such as "At the subsequent Board of Enquiry" and "Temper dash with Discretion" …'

November was busy with a mix of training and operational Jindivik flying both day and night, together with preparing for the forthcoming pilotless Meteor trials with WK800. In early November WK800 was launched with a safety pilot for air-testing and in late November I qualified as a Pitch Controller. However, I was 'Az' on 7th December for the first operational pilotless Meteor sortie for seven years. This was the 783rd pilotless Meteor sortie from Llanbedr, the last occasion having been on 8th December 1981.

In the hangar I'd looked with awe at the red and yellow Meteor with its enormous air intakes and high tail and thought about steering this powerful machine, pilotless, down the runway by remote control with a tiny joystick. The start of the take-off run was always 'anxious' because the Azimuth Controller's inputs had little effect because the left/right joystick sent commands to the rudder only. Only as the Meteor accelerated, increasing the airflow past the rudder, did the commands begin to bite. We had found that WK800 usually veered to the right. The surface wind could either compensate for or aggravate this tendency. Sometimes a slight left offset from the taxying pilot before he climbed out would assist the Azimuth Controller. We achieved four pilotless Radar Vector Miss Distance Indicator development Meteor sorties without a hitch before we ended the year on 23rd December with a Meteor training sortie.

1989

Early in the new year, pilotless Meteor sorties resumed without me for a couple of sorties as I was on the Operations Desk, deputising for the Operations Officer. The critical moments when 'Azimuth' works to get the target lined up on the centreline of the runway while Pitch eases the target into the landing attitude for touchdown at a suitable speed were made more difficult by the crosswind. From the Ops Desk I watched the Meteor approach and winced when the slightly heavy crosswind landing resulted in a wheel coming off and WK800 returning to the hangar once more for a few weeks.

Dark afternoons and wintry weather reduced the amount of flying and when someone suggested I should revive *Target*, I agreed. I canvassed contributions, particularly from the long-serving staff as Llanbedr's history was so unusual. Mike Fairfax-Rawlings of the Photographic Section produced

A fine study of Meteor U.16 WK800 taking off on 7th December 1988 at the start of the first pilotless Meteor sortie for seven years.

Meteor U.16 WK800 with RVMDI modifications.

interesting photos from his archives. For the 'down under' story of Jindivik, I was directed to Rob Nash of Aerospace Technologies of Australia who became an excellent and helpful source of information. Also Ben Dannecker, one of the Jindivik Target Controllers at Jervis Bay wanted to exchange news and views with Llanbedr Ops and both have continued to do so to this day.

From my word processor I went to the HQ photocopier helped by the ever-cheerful Sarah Tibbets until I had enough pages spread out on the Conference Room table to arrange and fold into 200-plus copies of an A4-sized amateurish station rag. In the serious part Manager Ian Smith wrote: 'Over the last year or so we have encouraged a growth in our operations with the aim of enhancing

the long-term future of the Establishment. As well as the normal Jindivik service we have carried out trials around the Isle of Wight, the Channel, around the coasts of Scotland and Gibraltar. The letters of appreciation I have received from our customers show the regard in which the Llanbedr service is held, so credit on all of your efforts.

'We have also seen considerable investment in the Establishment. The present contract has been extended until 1 July 1990. However, we have to face the unsettling period of bidding for the next contract period. The Ministry has already issued the "Invitation to Tender" to interested firms who will be visiting the site in April.'

Before pilot Roy Gamblin left to join British Aerospace he flew his last Canberra mission around the Highlands of Scotland with Vic Court in the rear seat. Vic recalled the flight: 'It was a beautifully clear but very windy March day which meant there'd be turbulence flying low level in the mountains. For over two hours I was shaken violently up and down in my ejection seat. Driving over cobblestones doesn't come near to describing the sensation. When good old George Casey, the Instrument Mechanic took the fatigue meter readings afterwards he nearly had a baby, never having seen such a score before through all his RAF career!'

In March, when Meteor U.16 WK800 was back on the line, the RVMDI trial resumed and in April I qualified as a Jindivik Navigator. Back on 'Az' for a Meteor sortie on 19th April, I had 'finger trouble' and steered into the barrier, thus condemning the Meteor to another spell in the hangar.

In April Group Captain Roger Beazley AFC FRAeS RAF became Commanding Officer of the Experimental Flight at RAE Farnborough and said: 'Llanbedr is a specialised unique sort of place and it often surprises people to find that Llanbedr aircrew, air traffic controllers and the airfield (less the sheep) are an integral part of the Experimental Flying Department. I shall keep the date of my downing a Jindivik earlier in my career to myself. Too many people at Llanbedr care about Jindiviks and that one might have been someone's pet!'

In June Vic Court climbed into the back of a Hawk T.1 for some high g trials to operate the camera for the culmination of a series of flights exploring the range of a pilot's head movements under increasing levels of sustained g. He explained: 'We mounted a small video camera in the front cockpit, looking at the pilot's head, with the camera controls in the rear cockpit. The limit in the Hawk was $8g$ and we had to explore levels from around 3 to $7g$. We wore g trousers and the "grunting" action had become second nature to me with the 3 or $4g$ regularly encountered in the Hawk. But $7g$ was different. Your "bone dome" is crushed onto your head, your oxygen mask has to be very tight to prevent it from being ripped from your face. Your arms are so heavy it is impossible to move them

Meteor U.16 WK800 veers off the Llanbedr runway after a heavy landing.

and you must remember to grunt like the clappers to keep blood flowing to your brain.

'I flew the 7*g* trial with Andy Carolan who was, as always, totally professional in his handling of the aircraft, managing to establish the turn after pulling a peak *g* level of 7.75*g*. What fun it was!'

In November Canberra B.2 WK128, carrying Hybrid targets (a variant of Stiletto), was on exercise on Royal Artillery Range Hebredes, crewed by Andy and Vic. They were taking off from Leuchars when a flock of black-headed gulls flew into the same airspace. Vic explained what happened next: 'Just after we left the ground there was a loud bang followed by the aircraft rolling and yawing. I couldn't tell how much because from the nav's seat you have a very poor view of the outside and no artificial horizon. I knew we must be very close to our safety speed (the speed above which the Canberra can fly on one engine). I sat there with my hand poised ready to pull the handle and leave the pilot to sort things out.

'After a few seconds Andy said he was considering clearing the wings but as the aircraft was still flying he decided not to. We struggled into the air and overflew the tower for them to check if they could see anything wrong. (At that stage we didn't know that several gulls had gone down the port engine and caused it to surge.) We were fortunate that the engine still put out sufficient power to get us airborne and didn't completely stall.

Aftermath: WK800 after suffering damage to its undercarriage as a result of the heavy landing shown on the opposite page.

'Andy did a brilliant job. He nursed the engine through the next several hours of flight while we diverted and burned off fuel. At one point we were asked to change our holding pattern because we were interfering with someone's TV. There we were in a sick aircraft, waiting to perform a virtual asymmetric landing (not the safest of Canberra operations) and someone was peeved about their TV viewing. They weren't to know of course!

'We finally landed OK and then it took me an hour to make the Stiletto safe and brief the fire crew about the hazards of the Stiletto. When we finally returned to our hotel after driving miles across the Highlands of Scotland the lads had a whip-round and bought us quite a lot of beer!'

Vic went on to do photo-chase work in the Hawk. When he eventually handed in his flying kit he said: 'I thought it was wonderful to have all these flying adventures as a civilian who had never been in the services or had any of the formal RAF aircrew training. When I started, Peter Shaw was the pilot who taught me most of my flying duties and always offered good advice and I went on to fly with many different pilots, and with most of them I thoroughly enjoyed it.'

WK800 suffers a barrier engagement after 'finger trouble'. Note the replacement starboard engine cowling from Meteor T.7 WA662, the colours contrasting with the drone scheme.

Andy Carolan (left) with Vic Court and a Hawk T.1 prior to a high *g* flight trial.

Chapter Seven

The 1990s

1990

With approval to hold a Families Day and Reunion obtained from the Farnborough Board of Management by Ian Smith, a small group of us met at The Vic to launch the Llanbedr Airfield Golden Jubilee enterprise.

There was an intensive week when RAE Llanbedr was tasked with providing successions of Jindivik targets on range for the NATO exercise 'Elder Forest' every day. After a busy week launching Jindiviks for a NATO exercise, Operations Officer Tony Townshend wrote a humorous insight for *Target* into one day of our 'war games' entitled:

A Sideways Look at RAE Llanbedr's Score in 'Elder Forest'

08.00 Hawk airborne to recce war zone. 30 foreign vessels disguised as fishing fleet encountered.

 –   Target Controller WM broke foot kick-starting crewroom clock. [I fell as I climbed to wind the clock, limiting me to the Navigator's seat for a few weeks!]

08.40 Jindivik airborne to intercept fighter that launched a missile. Jindi survived & RTB.

10.00 Jindivik airborne against another missile. Survived & RTB. Launch trolley not so keen, left runway, was caught trying to escape.

12.00 Three Belgian fishing boats anchored in middle of war zone for lunch and scallops.

12.30 Jindivik tries to desert. Controllers prevent escape. Locked in hangar and another Jindi brought out.

12.55 Reserve Jindi airborne, faces missile and survives encounter. RTB

14.20 Scrambled another Jindi to intercept a Tornado. It missed. RTB.

16.35 Yet another Jindi goes to war, evades fighter, obviously enjoying event and wants to go round again. Forced to land by the Controllers when getting low on fuel.

18.00 RAF throw in the towel & surrender. Awarded wooden spoon.

Final result: Llanbedr 5 – RAF nil.

Airfield staff were dismayed to learn that Airwork Services Ltd had lost the Llanbedr contract to FR Serco and they would once again have to suffer the down-sizing/redundancy/re-employment process. This time the redundancy notices were for 31st March 1991 and included our newest colleagues – pilot Chris Laidlaw-Bell and target controllers Tim Miles and Mike Webb. The new contractors invited us to re-apply for our jobs to start on 1st April 1991! FR Serco was jointly owned by FR Aviation and Serco; they operated RNAS Yeovilton, RAE West Freugh and RAF Swinderby and had just won contracts to operate RAF Woodvale and RAF Shawbury as well as RAE Llanbedr. Each contract was led by one or other of the two companies and at Llanbedr it was to be FR.

'Meteorific!' enthused ex-RAF pilot Derek Fitzsimmons on joining Operations and finding a Meteor in the fleet. He was a Vintage Pair Meteor pilot for the 1975 display season and was tasked to convert Hugh Skinner, the OC Flying at Llanbedr to the type: 'I went to Llanbedr with some trepidation to do this flying because the Gaskell/Ainsworth experience levels were well known. However they were in the smokers' crew-room most of the time and our paths hardly crossed!'

Derek returned to Llanbedr and flew the 'Gentleman's Carriage of the Skies': 'Flying this Meteor [WK800] is different. All you have to do is to make sure it doesn't crash whilst the company who were downing the drinks with you last night fly you around by remote control. Master Controller Dan Carter asks if you are ready for take-off, but before you answer he says, "Never mind, you're going anyway" and presses the CLIMB button to launch the Meteor. Also, now that Bob Gaskell

has finally retired, me and the luggage no longer finish up in the canopy because of his levelling-off technique!

'It's a privilege to fly this aircraft. Simulated emergencies such as loss of telemetry, loss of throttle control, loss of pitch and roll commands are practised to limits that can't be done with the Jindivik.'

When Meteor U.16 WH453 retired in the late summer, WK800 took over the role of training and development testing vehicle; and Anson T.21 VS562 (8021M) returned to be rebuilt by aircraft fitters Kevin Hobbs and Bob Frizell, assisted by Llanbedr Air Training Corps cadets, in a project sponsored by the local Maes Artro Aviation Museum.

Left: **Kevin Hobbs (right), Bob Frizell (left) with cadets and Avro Anson T.21 VS562.**

Below: **The Control Tower staff.**

Photographs on the opposite page:

Canberra B.2(TT) WK128 on approach to Llanbedr. *John Hale*

Devon C.2 XA880 over the Welsh countryside.

Meteor U.16 WK800 over the sands at Llanbedr. *John Hale*

1991

In March I had the pleasure of showing our vintage aircraft to the RAF's first female navigator when Flying Officer Anne-Marie Dawe arrived in an RAF Valley Hawk T.1. In April most of us were back in our jobs but there were farewells to Ian P Smith, who went to Airwork's head office, and also to Cath Brown, Irene Roberts, Meira Pierce, Gwylym Jones, Wil 'Cash' Davies, Danny Jenkins, 'Dick' Gear and Owen Hughes. The new Manager was George Smith, not a newcomer to the drone business since he was at RAE Aberporth when the first drone Firefly was launched.

I was working on the Golden Jubilee issue of *Target* when Frank Guard offered to persuade the printing branch at RAE Farnborough to print it for me, IN COLOUR. He asked how many copies would be needed and I multiplied our last issue by three, rounded up a bit and tried: 'A thousand copies, please?' He put me in touch with Harvey Mozley who said: 'Just let me know what you want in good time' and delivered.

On 14th May there were dreadful moments when a Jindivik hit the ground short of the runway and struck a parked car on returning from Aberporth Range. I was in the Navigator's seat and, under ATC's direction, I'd turned the Jindivik onto the final approach track while the Skipper flew it to intercept the correct glidepath. Control of A92-706 was then delegated to the Pitch and Azimuth Controllers to carry out a visual approach and landing. In the Control Cell the Skipper was reading off the RPM and airspeed and I monitored the track of the target. Range calls were interjected by the PAR controller. I was ready to resume azimuth control if the Jindivik were to 'go around' for some reason, but we expected the Jindivik to touch down and be fuelled off. Then my task would be completed apart from reporting to Aberporth that we had landed, closing down my console and completing my small share of the paperwork.

However, Jindivik A92-706 never reached the runway and suddenly we heard the Shepherd pilot reporting that it had crashed, hit a car and there was a fire. As he circled overhead in the Hawk we heard Sepp directing the fire engine and ambulance to a scene that the Skipper and I, listening in our darkened cell, visualised with horror and apprehension. 'We've landed, Aberporth, goodbye!' I reported brightly, to discourage them from asking questions that I feared to answer, and cut the link.

Leslie and Betty Cox, senior citizens on holiday from The Midlands, were in their parked car, facing the sea, when they heard the approaching Jindivik. It was losing height and looked very low, Leslie observed from his front seat. Betty was in the back. The Jindivik struck a tree, skidded along the ground and burst into flames heading for their car. Then it bounced just enough for the wing to pass over the car roof and the fuselage to pass over the bonnet, but the extended landing skid smashed into the engine. Although the car was briefly enveloped in flames the Coxes extricated themselves and ran from it.

From the air Sepp Pauli observed Betty running back towards the burning Jindivik and later discovered her purpose was to help the pilot, not knowing the Jindivik was pilotless!

With the fire engine and the ambulance came Airfield Nurse Alice Ash. Leslie Cox, who suffered one or two minor cuts, said afterwards: 'Alice Ash was an angel who steered us into the ambulance where we were whisked to the first aid unit at the airfield. She was so kind and consoling. While waiting for the doctor she phoned our relatives to assure them we were safe before the media could report the accident.'

Jindivik flying was suspended for over three months while a meticulous and lengthy Board of Enquiry was held. Every possible lesson was learned from the accident and stringent new mandatory procedures were introduced and practised regularly to make certain that this kind of accident would not, could not, ever be repeated. Jindivik losses or damage, whether caused by missiles, mishandling or technical faults on the runway or over clear areas of sea might be costly, but were to be accepted as an inevitable part of UAV operations. However, people and private property must not be endangered and future policy was to be that unless it was certain that UAVs could be landed safely on the airfield they were to be destroyed out at sea. New monitoring and back-up procedures would ensure in future that any shortfall due to human factors or faulty equipment was immediately identified and action taken to resolve it.

While awaiting clearance to resume flying Jindiviks, we kept our hands in flying training sorties with the manned Meteor, WK800, which provided the opportunity of flying our Golden Jubilee limited editions of Royal Mail aeronautical souvenir covers in an historic aircraft. On 21st June they were flown in a special compartment in the aircraft.

In August, when George Smith left, George Hobbs became Deputy Contract Manager/ Engineering Manager and also Acting Contract Manager. For *Target* he reviewed the situation in Llanbedr's Golden Jubilee year: 'Llanbedr's primary task is to provide aerial targets for the Aberporth Range and off-range work in the UK and overseas. The inventory of aircraft consists of:

A) Five Jindivik Mk 103B aircraft
B) Fourteen Jindivik Mk 4A airframes
C) Two Canberra B.2 aircraft modified to take:
   1) Rushton Towed Target System. Up to 30,000 ft of towing cable can be deployed to tow one of the following targets:
      i. Rushton Mk 3
      ii. Rushton low level height-keeper
      iii. MRTT
      iv. Range Proving Vehicle
   2) Supersonic Target – preset before take-off to give presentations up to 2.2 Mach and between 1,000 feet and 70,000 feet.
D) Two Hawk T.1s – these are used for tracking trials and shepherd duties for the Jindivik operation.
E) One Devon communications aircraft – this can also be used for tracking trials.
F) One Meteor U.16 – used for target controller training, fitted with a TV camera in the nose.
G) One Sea Vixen D.3 held in storage.

FUTURE DEVELOPMENTS:

We expect to see the Advanced Ground Station enter service this year. This is a computer-based ground control station using VDU displays.

For Jindivik Mk 4A the following systems are being developed:
a) Chaff and IR dispenser system for fitting in the wing-tips and in tows
b) The Hayes Universal Towed Target System
c) Missile Approach Warning System
A new order has been placed with ASTA for Jindivik Mk 4A Block 2 aircraft for delivery in 1995/6.'

Sir Michael F Cobham CBE, Chairman and Chief Executive of the FR Group PLC in his Foreword for *Target* wrote that the association between FR and Llanbedr Airfield 'goes back over many years. During the 1950s and 1960s Flight Refuelling Ltd, the founder company of FR Group, converted more than 200 Meteor F.4s and Meteor F.8s to the drone role, a large number of which saw service at Llanbedr – and incidentally, I was delighted to see one of the few remaining Meteors still flying operationally when I visited Llanbedr. Subsequently the company was responsible for the conversion of the Sea Vixen FAW.2 aircraft to the drone role. Flight Refuelling also developed the Canberra towed-target system and designed and manufactured both the winches and targets incorporated therein.'

Gordon Brown wrote: 'One thing has never changed. That is the pride that people take in being part of Llanbedr which has always enjoyed an enviable reputation throughout the aviation community for its high standards.'

During the year, funding for Sea Vixen operations was withdrawn and so XP924 was grounded and joined XS577 in storage. In the autumn ex-RAF Wing Commander Phil Cutts was appointed Contract Manager and we held our Families Day at the airfield followed by a Reunion Party on Shell Island. In one of the hangars we exhibited all the entries for the Golden Jubilee logos and motifs design competitions and entertained the winning pupils, their parents and teachers from local schools. Prizes were presented to: **7 Years** – 1st: Cari Wyn Owen (Ysgol Talsarnau); Highly Commended: Bethan Williams, David Key, Huw Morgan, Rachel Patton (all of Ysgol Talsarnau). **8 Years** – 1st: Elenid Price (Ysgol Talsarnau); 2nd: Carys Maxwell (Ysgol Tanycastell, Harlech). **9 Years** – 1st: Gwynfor Evans (Ysgol Aruduwy); 2nd: Claire Joanne Rayner (Ysgol Talsarnau). **10 Years** – 1st: Emma

Gregory (Ysgol Cefn Coch, Penrhyndeu-dreth); 2nd: Clark Norman (Ysgol Dyffryn Ardudwy); 3rd: Emma Howie (Ysgol Tancastell). **11 Years** – 1st: Steven Lee Williams (Ysgol Talsarnau); 2nd: James Wright (Ysgol Dyffryn Ardudwy); 3rd: Julian John (Ysgol Tanycastell); Highly Commended: Nicholas Beazley, Farnborough. Staff winners were Gary Jones' design for souvenir coffee mugs and polo shirts, Tony Townshend's design for the souvenir Royal Mail covers and Andy McNally's humorous design for souvenir T-shirts and mugs.

During the year a third member of the Fairfax-Rawlings family joined the RAE when Timothy, son of Llanbedr Airfield Photographer Mike, began his electronic engineering apprenticeship. His mother Pauline had just begun her fourth tour of employment in the target service, working in Tech Control. Pauline was Secretary to the Technical Manager for six years before marrying Mike a fortnight before his detachment to Woomera where she became Secretary to the Manager at RAAF Evetts Field in 1968. On return to the UK Pauline was Secretary to the Officer-in-Charge at Llanbedr before resigning to have a second child. Mike and Pauline totalled 37 years of target service before Tim began his contribution.

Tudor Rowlands (Air Radio) and Janice Rees (Engineering Secretary) returned to Llanbedr for second 'tours' during the year. Following the death of his wife, retired Store-Keeper Charlie Harris passed away and I was grateful to their elder daughter, Hilda, for the use of Charlie's meticulous notes and cuttings in his scrapbook.

1992

'Best thing I ever did!' said Maggie Roberts in January on becoming Llanbedr's first female Air Traffic Control Officer at the age of 25. Local girl Maggie had worked in Stores but when ex-RAF Flight Observer Peter T S Brown became a part-time Target Controller, she replaced him as part-time Air Traffic Control Assistant. Maggie was promised a passenger flight in the Devon C.2 but it was unserviceable and requisitions for Devon parts continually crossed her desk.

Eventually Maggie boarded for a flight to A&AEE Boscombe Down, but just before take-off the aircraft became unserviceable again and taxied back. At lunchtime Maggie

ATCO Maggie Roberts on Airfield Inspection.

saw Dai Ynys working on the Devon, with parts spread around him. Later when she went to board the Devon again, Dai greeted her with a screw and a washer, pretending he didn't know where they fitted in: 'He thought this was funny, but I was terrified!' said Maggie who went on to become Deputy to Senior Air Traffic Control Officer Reg Jarvis.

On 31st January A92-722 became the first UK Jindivik to reach 200 flights.

In May the *DRA News* commented that 'Simulated Trading, with its currency "the purple pound" is under way. This will be a testing time for DRA staff if we are to achieve our goal of convincing Parliament and the Treasury that we will be in a fit state to embark on Full Trading by April 1993.' The objective was to create a leaner, more efficient DRA at reduced cost on fewer sites. Soon after this the sign-writers, the printers, the stationers and the T-shirt suppliers had to get busy again as DRA Llanbedr suddenly became T&EE Llanbedr under the wing of the Directorate General of Testing and Evaluation when there was more streamlining and concentration of activities on fewer larger establishments.

When the IT6 contingent was broken up Frank Guard and Brian Luff moved to Pyestock and continued to support the work of Llanbedr under the authority of DGTE Aberporth. Frank Guard explained: 'The core activities at Farnborough were being taken over by DERA and Llanbedr came under the wing of DGTE with Aberporth as the direct tasking authority. With the DGTE hierarchy and MoD(PE) Controller Air staff at Boscombe Down, supervision of Aberporth and target operations was convenient with "Release to service authority" and Engineering Authority for Llanbedr aircraft more or less under one roof.

'Around this time there was a revival of the ambition to fly Jindivik target aircraft out of Benbecula in The Hebrides. New Jindivik Control facilities were being developed by Llanbedr staff and GEC-Marconi with computer-based control systems and software that could be fitted into a two-storey portable cabin as well as the established Control Cells in the Tower. With new institutions in control

of the old RAE and MoD(PE) functions, it was a mammoth task to obtain the Airworthiness and Flight Clearances. Phil Williams pulled many irons out of the fire to obtain formal design approval for the new computer system.'

On 14th May the attendance at St Peter's Church after his death indicated the respect and affection of the local community for Derek Newton, an ex-Operations Officer of Llanbedr airfield where he had served for over 25 years.

In August, in Australia, Frank Cranston reviewed Jindivik and its potential for *The Canberra Times*: 'Jindivik's usual role is to tow targets for aircraft and anti-aircraft gunners to attack using either visual, radar or heat-seeking guidance. In other attacks missiles are set to miss and their passage is photographed. Occasionally a Jindivik has not side-stepped smartly enough and has come under direct fire.'

Cranston said that Jindivik had another role 'attacking' a warship from very low altitude just above the waves, simulating a fast pass by a hostile aircraft or a missile attack. Also Jindivik could streak past a Rapier or RBS-70 missile battery to exercise the operators. As Jindivik becomes faster and climbs higher it is a better training aid for pilots of the latest fighters. Jindivik also held promise as an autonomously operating over-the-horizon vehicle unlimited by the current 180 km and line-of-sight restrictions. Carrying special cameras and sensors, Jindivik could be developed to operate over distances up to 2,000 km to sweep coastlines and maritime approaches. There were numerous battlefield uses for Jindivik, suggested Cranston: battlefield surveillance, flare-dropping, electronic eavesdropping and many more.

On 30th October the 6,000th UK Jindivik flight was made by A92-737. This was a development flight and the Skipper was Bob Gaskell. He, along with some of the technical staff, had been involved with the first and now the 6,000th Jindivik sorties. Those involved with the latter sortie were Alun Jones, Ray Tyson, John W Andrews, Phil J Williams, Ron J Telfer, George Hobbs, Des Roberts, Chris Smith, Gordon V Brown, George Brown, Dave Lumb, and John S

Jones, all of whom were employed continuously at Llanbedr throughout. Gwyn L Jones, Charlie Meadows, Sim Oakley, Tudor Rowlands and Keith Unwin also saw both sorties, but had worked elsewhere for intervening periods before returning to Llanbedr.

Ex-RAF pilot Jon Webb and ex-Royal Navy Observer Greg Aldred joined the Operations Section during the year while long-serving Motor Transport mechanic William Henry Evans and long-serving Chargehand Fitter Goronwy Wynn Davies retired from the Motor Transport section.

With retirement in view Airfield Medical Officer 'Doc Gareth' handed over to colleague Dr Malcolm Hickey. Dr Gareth Williams had followed his father Dr R W Williams ('Dr Bach') into the position. As a

Above: **Ops and Technical staff after the 6,000th UK Jindivik sortie.**

Below: **Technical staff with Jindivik A92-737.**

young medical student with a temporary job at the airfield Gareth would tell the switchboard: 'Don't forget to call me in an emergency as well as Dad!' As a young boy Gareth had accompanied his father on calls so as to open and close the many gates for him, said his wife Dorothy who continued serving the airfield as Relief Nurse into the 21st century. There were tributes to 'Doc Gareth's' long service to Llanbedr airfield with presentations being made to him by Gordon Brown and Bob Gaskell on behalf of Airfield and Operations personnel.

In his Manager's letter for *Target* just before Christmas, Phil Cutts wrote: 'Of the many changes we have experienced, perhaps the least understandable have been the numerous changes to the NAME of the establishment! However, we have been Test and Evaluation Establishment Llanbedr for some months now, so perhaps these changes are over! The 6,000th UK Jindivik flight and the introduction of Jindivik Mk 4 into operational service are achievements in which we may take some pride. As a newcomer to the team I have been very impressed with the willingness of "old hands" to pass on their experience, and also the enthusiasm they display for their specialisation. I believe it is this combination of experience and enthusiasm which makes Llanbedr such a special place, also for the community spirit which binds them together.'

1993

'The ubiquitous Advanced Ground Station seems to have taken us back to square one with the addition of two Vega Cantley tracking radars!' observed Derek Whitehead.

In February Llanbedr's second home-built Jindivik, 'Llan 2' made a successful maiden flight, followed by operational sorties as the aircraft earned its keep during a busy summer and accomplished 66 sorties before suffering Cat 5 damage in 1996 on a night take-off.

Above: **A retirement presentation to 'Doc Gareth' Williams (centre) by Bob Gaskell (left) and Gordon Brown (right).**

Below: **LLAN2, the second 'home-built' Jindivik.**

Llanbedr said goodbye to two long-serving institutions when Bob Gaskell and the 'Farnborough Ferry' Piper Navajo Chieftain were retired. Bob's service at Llanbedr totalled 35 years while the 'Farnborough Ferry' service, based at Farnborough, had run since 1946. We dined out Bob and his wife Mavis at the Castle Cottage restaurant and because his summing-up of any situation was always the same, we presented him with a plaque on which was inscribed: 'It was all just a piece

of piss' We recalled that Bob would observe irritably: 'The wind's getting up, damn it,' or 'Bloody cunimbs developing'. If someone reassured him that the Jindivik would probably be safely back in the hangar before the bad weather arrived, he'd respond: 'I'm not bothered about the f****** Jindivik. I'm bothered about my golf this evening!' Following Bob's departure, Tim Miles took on the position of DOCFU (Deputy Officer-in-Charge of Flying (Unmanned).

In June our longest-serving Jindivik, A92-722, retired in style with a 'splash-down' into Cardigan Bay. The Jindivik was destroyed on its 264th sortie after being hit by a Rapier surface-to-air missile. Another Jindivik (A92-740) was brought safely back to base with a damaged tailplane and elevator, illustrating once again how sturdy and resilient was the Jindivik.

1994

Defence Costs Study 4 proposed the formation of a single agency to contain all MoD non-nuclear science and technology organisations *including DGTE* by April 1995. Llanbedr was reassured there was still a firm contract for the supply of 18 new Jindiviks, which demonstrated the MoD's continued commitment to the Llanbedr target service. FR Serco was awarded a two-year extension to operate T&EE Llanbedr until March 1996. It was also announced that because our sole remaining Meteor was running out of fatigue life, a two-year project to equip the Hawk T.1 to fly in the drone role, albeit with a safety pilot, had begun.

When Harry Warburton's son, Corporal Barry Warburton, was killed in Bosnia while defusing anti-personnel devices, there was much sympathy as the Warburtons were a popular family and Harry had kept The Vic for many years both during and after the Second World War. Barry's body was flown home in an RAF Hercules that landed at Llanbedr airfield on 29th March. With full military honours he was transported to St Peter's Church, just a few yards from The Vic in Llanbedr village, for the funeral. Colonel Ian Daniels, Commanding Officer of 33 Regiment of the Royal Engineers said: 'Corporal

Warburton was an excellent soldier, an outstanding NCO and very popular.'

There was another obituary on the other side of world following the death of Ian Bowman Fleming. *The Canberra Times* announced: 'Father of Jindivik dies. The principal designer of the jet aircraft that has been in production longer than any other died in John James Hospital, aged 80. He was one of Australia's leading aircraft designers.'

At Llanbedr the new computerised Control Cell using fibre-optics (the AGS) was being developed to replace the old 'steam' cells and a portable version would remove one of the major limitations on Jindivik – that of confining it to Llanbedr and Aberporth Range. Ground crews and target controllers started familiarising themselves with the AGS using the faithful old workhorse Meteor U.16 to prove and re-prove the AGS system.

In April we learned that two eras of historic aviation would end when the experimental flying activities at our traditional 'parent unit' Farnborough, also Bedford, were transferred to Boscombe Down. Experimental flying at Bedford had begun during the Second World War, whereas at Farnborough (a longtime 'parent unit' to Llanbedr) it dated back to the end of the 19th century.

During the year our bosses (the FR Group) celebrated their 60th anniversary of the founding of Flight Refuelling Ltd by pioneer aviator Sir Alan Cobham. 'FR' had gone from strength to strength in the hands of Sir Alan and his team, and then under his son Michael. In tribute to them the name was changed to Cobham PLC.

In May Len Morgan retired from flying to continue as a Target Controller. Devon C.2 XA880 was replaced by a younger 'twin', Piper Navajo Chieftain ZF521. For Len's (and the Devon's) last flight, he and Steve Ives led a formation flypast with the Hawk T.1s and Meteor U.16 WK800. On landing we greeted Len on the tarmac with a bottle of champagne to celebrate his 42-year flying career and visiting MP, Elfyd Griffiths, added his congratulations. According to Len the Devon was: 'A lovely old lady, reliable, stable, responsive, never seriously let me down. It had leather seats and you could smoke in it – unless the priming pump was leaking!

The Piper Navajo Chieftain 'Farnborough Ferry' (last visit) and crew, with Derek Fitzsimmons (left) and about-to-retire Bob Gaskell (2nd from right). The inscription on the aircraft reads, Final Ferry To West Coast 1946-1993 'So Sad'.

Jindivik A92-740 makes its way back to Llanbedr having suffered notable damage to its rear fuselage and starboard elevator as a result of a missile strike during a presentation over Cardigan Bay.

Above: **The new computerised Control Cell during development in 1994.**

Below: **The traditional pilot's retirement ceremony. Len is released after a dowsing by fire hoses to share champagne with colleagues.**

Photographs on the opposite page:

A 'clean' Jindivik Mk 4 A92-804 flies in the Outer Hebrides for the first time.

Venerable trio: Len Morgan and Steve Ives in Devon C.2 XA880 lead Meteor U.16 WK800 and Hawk T.1 XX170 (on loan from 234 (R) Squadron) in a flypast to mark Len's and the Devon's retirement from flying.

Meteor U.16 WK800 is fitted with drop tanks for Benbecula Ops.

I shall always remember when the weather was bad at Llanbedr but the tops of all the mountains were standing up spectacularly from a level sheet of cloud.'

Jindivik A92-809 was loaned to ASTA as their reference aircraft for the new purchase of 18 Jindivik Mk 4A 900 series aircraft and in May George Hobbs returned to Australia to instruct ASTA personnel on the necessary assembly and testing procedures. In June at Llanbedr a Jindivik was flown on the AGS system for the first time, with an old 'steam' cell prepared as stand-by. It wasn't needed and after more Jindivik flights on AGS it was time to rehearse the portable system with a view to deploying Jindivik to the Royal Artillery Range Hebrides.

Benbecula was on our minds throughout the year as the Navajo Chieftain ferry aircraft and road transports went to and from Benbecula airfield, preparing for the Llanbedr detachment. We familiarised ourselves with the new mobile Control Cell positioned abeam the Target runway and the new Azimuth control trailer before they were taken to Benbecula. Rosters, travel arrangements and hotel bookings were made. Staff and crews were to rotate between Llanbedr and Benbecula, courtesy of the Navajo Chieftain.

After several proving flights with the manned Meteor, the first flight of Jindivik in the Hebrides took place during the evening of 21st September. Shepherded by Jon Webb

115

in Hawk T.1 XX160, Jindivik A92-804 made a successful 40-minute flight 'due very much to the initiatives and hard work put in by Llanbedr staff,' reported Frank Guard.

During the year, Sea Vixen D.3 XS577 was blanked off and parked outside.

1995

The name DERA (Defence Evaluation & Research Agency) was proposed for the new single agency and this gave rise to jokes about whether it would rhyme with 'dearer' or 'terror' – the latter won the day! Llanbedr continued providing a target service for Aberporth Range and other customers including the Royal Navy, the Royal Artillery Range in the Hebrides (RARH) and West Freugh in Scotland. The fleet included Jindivik Mk 103Bs and Mk 4As, Hawk T.1s, Canberra B.2(TT)s, the Meteor U.16 and a Navajo Chieftain. The Jindiviks were able to carry two targets. These could be simple infra-red flares or the more sophisticated Semi-Active Radar Targets for radar-homing missiles.

The Hawks served as 'skin' targets for tracking trials as well as shepherding duties. There was a plan to drone two Hawks as MDTA (Manned Drone Training Aircraft) for controller training as the Meteor U.16 was heading for retirement. The two Canberra B.2(TT)s could be equipped with Rushton towed target systems or the supersonic targets (Stiletto and the Hybrid series) as required. The Rushton winch allowed for infra-red or radar targets to be towed up to 30,000 feet behind the Canberra while the supersonic targets were launched at medium altitude from under the wing of the Canberra. The Navajo Chieftain was mostly used for communications and deploying crews between the Air Flight Ranges units.

1996

Friday 16th August was a very sad day for OPS when we learned that our colleague Steve Ives, aged 54, had died at home in Llanbedr village on his return from a short stay in hospital. We drove over to his family home in Cambridgeshire for the funeral and then we held a Memorial Service in St Peter's Church,

Llanbedr in November during which the John McGee poem 'High Flight' was read out.

Brian Fortune, Principal Flight Test Engineer of Rolls-Royce Military Aero Engines, visited Llanbedr to fly as an observer in the Shepherd aircraft when the Viper 201C turbojet intended for the Jindivik 900 series was flight-tested in Jindivik A92-803.

Ex-RAF navigator Dick Pittaway joined OPS in November and we found that Jindivik was not the first unpiloted aircraft with which he had been associated. During a practice combat mission with F-16s over the Nevada Desert his Tornado GR.1 formated on another Tornado GR.1 and the pair flew over the desert floor at 100 feet for 30 miles. When they approached a mountain range the leading aircraft flew straight into it while Dick's aircraft pulled up and over it. After landing back at Nellis, Dick and his pilot learned that the crashed Tornado had been pilotless as the crew had ejected earlier after loss of control!

Sea Vixen D.3 XP924 was on offer for sale as scrap. Ex-Navy Flight Observer/Target Controller Greg Aldred 'had spent some 2,000 hours in the "coal hole" (Observer's position) in Sea Vixens, surviving hundreds of deck landings by day and night and numerous excursions over foreign lands, not all friendly, and I had developed a fondness for this aircraft.' De Havilland jet aircraft enthusiast Gwyn Jones decided on a rescue operation assisted by Marcus Edwards, an ex-Navy Sea Vixen pilot who, according to Greg Aldred 'had given me some heart-stopping moments as his Observer, in the past. The MoD accepted Gwyn's offer and after much discussion between Gwyn (De Havilland Aircraft), the CAA, Llanbedr and other agencies concerned with restoration and operation of vintage aircraft, it was decided that XP924 could be made airworthy again. Several Llanbedr groundcrew gave up their weekends to work on the Sea Vixen.'

During the year Jindiviks A92-812 and A92-811 were shot down, 'Llan 2' crashed on take-off at night due to a trolley gyro fault and the first flight of A92-901 took place. Derek Whitehead, Charlie Meadows, Alun Jones and Bob Major retired and Relief Nurse Jean Hartley left.

1997

In the spring Sea Vixen D.3 XP924 was airworthy and ready for the airshow circuits. OC Flying Sepp Pauli climbed up into the familiar offset cockpit to fly it once more. With a farewell pass over the airfield, '924 headed south and was delivered to its new base at Swansea Airport.

In May, Phil Cutts reviewed recent events at Llanbedr: 'We've had a busy year with an extensive development programme (in addition to all the operational trials) in support of the new batch of Jindivik aircraft in manufacture in Australia. The new telecommand/telemetry systems were first test flown in the Meteor and later in a Jindivik Mk 4 800 series. With the run-up to the first test flight of a Jindivik Mk 4A 900 series this programme has been against extremely tight

Len Morgan (left) with Steve Ives.

Jindivik Mk 4 A92-803 with Viper 201C. Left to right: John Roberts, Ken Griffith, Iain Palmer, Mike Fisk (atop the Jindivik), Tim Miles, Dan Carter and Brian Fortune.

The 'morning after' Llan 2's night-time crash on take-off.

Charlie Meadows.

time constraints at every step. Congratulations on a job very well done.'

Under the Staff Suggestion Scheme, Senior Technical Officer Phil Williams received a Ministry of Defence award for 'Inventive and dedicated work carried out personally to allow all Llanbedr drone aircraft to fly on a single standard of software on the Advanced Ground System.'

In October Frank Guard retired from duty. He recalled earlier days: 'When some 20 more Mk 4 Jindiviks were ordered, built (on new jigs) and delivered to Llanbedr, George Hobbs played a sterling part in the build and

clearance task and his expertise supported Eric Baker (Air Arm 5) in convincing customers and our masters of the continuing need for UAVs and the effectiveness of Jindivik in this role.

'When we lost about eight Jindiviks in just over a year to live shots on the Range we had to review the allowable attack patterns and tighten up on procedures to reduce the risk of losing our costly UAV targets. The proposal to use Llanbedr's Canberra/Stiletto facilities in the Far East was prevented by political complications but we did modify our second Canberra to carry two Stilettos. The project to drone two Hawks was cancelled.

'I was fond of the Llanbedr people and protective of their work and performance and they always "produced the goods" in spite of the periodic contract changeover threats.

'Between 1991 and 1997, the plethora of changes of the hierarchy and tasking authorities was most unfortunate and I would like a pound for the number of times we, like you at Llanbedr, had to brief new people about these unique target facilities, their operations and needs. There were so many good people involved in the Llanbedr/Aberporth activities, not forgetting Idwal Edwards (Aberporth Senior Staff) for his wise management and support for Llanbedr.'

One Jindivik was lost during the year on a development flight. From Mynedd Rhiw Mike J Still retired after 31 years and also Mrs Ellen Girwen after 20 years at this lonely outpost. John W Andrews, John E Evans, Frank Kelleher, Bob McReady, John Owen, and Cadwallader Williams also retired from Llanbedr during the year.

1998

With the departure of Phil Cutts and the granting of another (ten-year) contract to FRA Serco, George Hobbs became Contract/Engineering Manager and in February Sir Michael Knight KCB AFC FRAeS (the new Chairman of Cobham PLC) made a flying visit to Llanbedr now that it was 'safely retained in FRA Serco hands'.

Around this time Ben Dannecker wrote that Jindivik flying in Australia was to cease in the summer but they were glad that the UK MoD had bought the design rights for Jindivik. The first launch of the MQM-107E

The MQM-107E Kalkara, procured to replace Jindiviks in Australia. Courtesy of Ben Dannecker

Kalkara, the replacement for Jindivik in Australia, was expected in early 1999.

At the end of February Gareth Jones (Labour Pool) left after 37 years of service, David 'Dai Llandanwg' Williams (Driver) after 25 years, Ellen Coulson (Storekeeper) after 14 years and Canteen Manager Sheila Hayden after ten years. Cook Michelle Davies left to have her baby Jack after six years at Llanbedr. At the end of March Driver Emlyn Owens left after 32 years, Administration Manager Danica Hughes left after 22 years and Maurice Hughes (Leading Firefighter) left after 18 years. We learned that Arthur Pearcy (a past ATC assistant and aviation historian) had died.

At the beginning of April Engineering Administrator Bethan Jones (whose father had been a winch operator in the days of No.5 CAACU) was promoted to Administration Manager and moved from the hangar to Administration HQ. Bethan was a Wages Clerk in 1977 and then clerk typist for the Technical Manager 'Dusty Rhodes'. Bethan was grateful to Chief Engineer Bill 'The Bees' Jones 'because he didn't just give me something to type, he'd explain what it meant!' When Shorts lost the contract to Airwork, Bethan started working for George Hobbs: 'On the first day he was discussing technical details with someone and when this was interrupted by a call from the MoD he just switched to another subject and also dictated. He had an incredible wealth of detailed information and I remember thinking then – will I cope?'

Over Easter Sepp Pauli and Greg Aldred planned to repeat their 1997 venture ferrying Canberra B(I)8 G-BXMO (ex-WT327) from DRA Bedford across the Atlantic via the Azores to new owners in the United States. However to deliver Canberra N40UP to California they planned to fly the Northern route via Iceland. On 8th April they took off from Bedford and were heading for Keflavik when their problems started with the failure of a booster pump. Fortunately their most convenient diversion was Llanbedr, just about to stand down for Easter. Greg remembered their unscheduled arrival back at their home base: 'Although they were just packing up for the long weekend, the lads in the hangar stayed behind to help. The Federal Aviation Administration and the sponsor flew in to get the problem fixed and between them they got us going again.'

During April George Brown (Electrical) retired after 41 years of service and David Henry 'Dai Penrhyn' Jones (Motor Transport Driver) retired after 28 years. Avionics Chargehand W Tudor Rowlands moved on to RAF Valley after working at Llanbedr from 1958 to 1966, 1973 to 1976 and 1984 to 1998.

In Australia an era ended on 26th June for the Royal Australian Navy with the last flight of an unmanned Jindivik at the Jervis Bay Range facility after 35 years. The Jindivik target-towing service had served the Royal Aus-tralian Navy, the Royal Australian Air Force and the Royal New Zealand Air Force but was being replaced because there was no suitable runway available in Western Australia where half of the Navy fleet was located. The replacement target – Kalkara (storm bird) – had a rocket-assisted motor and did not require a runway for take-off. 'I had the honour of throttling shut and landing the last Jindi to fly in Oz,' reported Den Dannecker

In July the local spotters at Llanbedr saw (and heard the 'bluenote' of) a Hawker Hunter FGA.9. Shortages in the RAF Hawk fleet reduced the Llanbedr fleet of three Hawk T.1s to just one, so Hunter FGA.9 XE601 was loaned by Boscombe Down for a year to help with the shepherding task.

The time was approaching for Sepp Pauli to cease flying military jets so Jon Webb took over as OC Flying and Operations Manager. Ex-RAF Buccaneer and Tornado navigator Paul Wilson joined OPS to become a UAV Controller and Deputy Operations Officer. Jim Shewring (Ground Electronics) retired after 35 years and Graham Biswell (Technical Assistant) retired after 29 years.

In November Hangar Foreman Desmond Roberts retired after 41 years. Also in Novem-

Hawker Hunter FGA.9 flown by Jon Webb.
Courtesy of Roman Schneller

'Good Show' certificates for 'hooley' controllers. The author of this book is third from the right.

ber, Peter Cox flew in from Australia to continue flying Jindiviks. An ex-Royal Australian Navy McDonnell A-4G Skyhawk pilot, he left the sea in 1978 to work at Jervis Bay and had 'skippered' the last two Australian Jindivik sorties. The penultimate sortie was for a missile firing by HMAS *Newcastle* and the final Australian Jindivik flight was a demonstration for Families Day. Peter and his wife Sue, an ex-Royal Australian Navy servicewoman, left their farm in the care of their sons to enable Peter to continue as a UAV controller at Llanbedr. He soon noted one obvious difference at Llanbedr: 'You don't have to clear the runway of kangaroos before launching a Jindivik!'

Jindivik A92-737, shot down by a Sea Dart surface-to-air missile, was the only one to be lost during 1998. Of the 190 Jindivik sorties flown 28 were (14 presentations of) 'Twin Jindiviks' and the very successful 'Echenies' flight trials at Aberporth, using Jindivik, continued into 1999.

1999

The 7,000th UK Jindivik flight took place early in the year and then on 5th March we had an interesting 'hooley' during an operational firing sortie. I was the Jindivik Navigator and had just completed streaming the towed target to 200 feet when a few things seemed to go pear-shaped for no apparent reason,

although it was later diagnosed as a severe lightning strike. Before any missiles had been fired our Jindivik appeared to have a power failure followed by an engine flame-out. The Skipper achieved a successful relight but I didn't know the status of the tow as I had lost my video picture and the telemetry wasn't making sense. We soon found this was not the only bit of mayhem and cancelled the firing.

The Shepherd aircraft joined up to inspect the Jindivik and reported the flaps were down. The Skipper tried unsuccessfully to retract them. Sepp confirmed the tow was still there but it refused my attempts to be brought in, wound out or jettisoned. Then the landing skid defied the Skipper's attempts to deploy it. After consultations with the Master Controller and George Hobbs, we conducted a slow-speed handling check and brought the Jindivik back to Llanbedr. With no 'undercarriage' and a target tow streamed out behind, the Jindivik was handed to the 'Sights' controllers out on the airfield for the approach and landing – 'using an untried approach and landing technique. The crew are commended for the cool and professional approach to this multi-faceted emergency and are awarded a

Director of Flying "Good Show"' said our citation.

In June, when the news got around that Jimmy James was travelling from Australia to revisit Llanbedr airfield, where he had served in the 1950s, the planned get-together grew into a reunion of around 50 senior ladies and gentlemen who were entertained to drinks and a buffet luncheon by the Llanbedr Airfield Golden Jubilee Association.

Following the Strategic Defence Review, cost-saving and the requirement to charge for trials led to reductions in manpower, overheads, equipment and support services. Trials requirements were managed individually as a project with a manager, the customer being charged for the use of personnel and equipment.

The majority of Britain's ground, sea and air-launched weapons systems at the end of the 20th century had been tested over Cardigan Bay, mostly using Llanbedr's target systems including the Jindivik or the Canberra with its supersonic Stiletto or towed target systems such as Rushton and low level height-keeping targets. The Jindivik was mostly required for air-to-air missile firings using IR and SART decoy tows.

High-speed cameras in the wing-tips provided miss distance and missile intercept trajectory information. The AMPOR (Aircraft/ Missile Proximity Optical Recorder) system included WRETAR (Weapons Research Establishment Target Aircraft Recorder) cameras. Each had either 'fish-eye' or rearward-looking lenses and enough film for 24 seconds' recording. Time coding formats enabled correlation of data. The Jindivik also had two ARMS (Advanced Radar Missile Scorer System) developed by Cambridge Consultants (UK) and with the need for more sophisticated decoys to keep up with weapon seeker technology, MOSART (Modulated Output Semi-Active Radar Target) was also being developed. Weapons able to identify the decoy and move on to the main target would probably signal the end of Jindivik's usefulness.

After 22 years as a pilot and target controller at Llanbedr it was Len Morgan's turn to retire and devote more time to family and his golf, while from the hangars three more long-serving members of staff who had also worked with Jindiviks in Australia also retired. They were Ron Telfer, Sim Oakley (1958-66, 1973-76, 1987-99) and Gwyn L Jones (1955-66, 1975-99). No Jindiviks were lost during the year.

A Jindivik night-time take-off.

Chapter Eight

The 21st Century

2000

Anticipating the appointment of a new Contract Manager to relieve George Hobbs, a party was planned to celebrate 'Mr Jindivik's' retirement on his 65th birthday. Long-standing friends and colleagues were invited and the arrangements made. However, when no appointment was made to replace him the party became a 'non-retirement' birthday party instead!

On my own 65th birthday OPS and Air Traffic Control dined me out right royally. A Jindivik plaque, Welsh crystal glasses, a Caithness vase with dolphins and a sea blue paperweight remind me of my dozen-plus years of being in a unique UAV crew at a historic airfield.

Wing Commander Keith Grumbley, A/D Air Operations pointed out that 'although there are enough Jindiviks to keep us going for another ten years or so, the replacement is beginning to exercise people. UAVs are sexy right now and Llanbedr has an ideal coastal location from which to mount test programmes for these gadgets.'

'Best firework display I've ever seen. It was very impressive watching Jindivik night operations,' said Paul Whitelegg, the new Contract Manager. Born in Cardiff, Paul was an ex-RAF Engineering Officer who came to Llanbedr with over 20 years of senior engineering management experience, most recently as FRA's Deputy Contract Manager of the Nimrod Major Servicing Unit at RAF Kinloss. Paul and his wife Sue, who have four children, had just settled in when, as he noted, 'I had to stand up in front of everyone and announce redundancies.'

In September the ex-Luftwaffe Alpha Jet ZJ645, one of 12 acquired by NewDERA, became operational and replaced the last Hawk T.1 around the time that Gary Jones lost his valiant battle with cancer. On learning of his fatal diagnosis Gary had continued working for as long as possible and in *Target* he thanked the workforce for supporting his fund-raising efforts for the Gwynedd Hospice at Home, saying: 'It is a comfort to know, when the sky above looks dark, the gloom is soon lifted with the help and support of friends and work colleagues. I thank you all and don't forget – GIVE IT MAX!'

2001 Diamond Jubilee Year

In January the MoD appointed Sir John Egan (who led BAA and Jaguar to success in the private sector) as Chairman of NewDERA to work with Chief Executive Sir John Chisholm to take 75 per cent of the agency into the private sector as a Public Private Partnership.

Recent advances with UAVs included a General Atomics RQ-1 Predator selecting and destroying a test target with a Hellfire anti-armour missile and a Northrop Grumman Global Hawk achieving a non-stop flight of around 7,500 miles from Edwards Air Force Base in California across the Pacific Ocean to Australia. On the civil side the VTOL Yamaha RMAX Aero Robot has been earning its keep on agricultural tasks in Japan.

In the UK several military UAVs have been adapted to extend their capability, including the BAE Systems Phoenix used by the Army for surveillance. 'Observer' technology was being developed by Cranfield Aerospace and QinetiQ with both military and civil applications in mind. The 'Watchkeeper' programme was to provide an all-weather long-

The A150 Airship N156LG at Llanbedr.

endurance tactical UAV and DERA demonstrated that Predator imagery can be provided to the cockpit of a Jaguar and that a fighter pilot could direct a small group of autonomous UCAVs from the cockpit.

In April it was reported that ASRAAM was indefinitely delayed because the MoD was not satisfied with its performance. The Advanced Short Range Air-to-Air Missile was overdue to replace the AIM-9 Sidewinder (in service for 25 years) and was to be fitted to RAF Tornado F.3s and Harrier GR.9s, Royal Navy Sea Harrier FA.2s and eventually to RAF Eurofighter Typhoons. Already over two years late when the announcement was made, ASRAAM was apparently still beset with hardware and software problems.

The 'aircraft spotters lay-by' overlooking the airfield became more popular than ever when A 150 Airship N156LG of the Lightning Group was based at Llanbedr for several weeks for the third phase of a Remote Minefield Detection System Technology Demonstration Programme (REMIDS TDP) that required the flight-testing of two sensors under study for detecting minefields over wide areas at altitudes of at least 1,000 feet. Foot-and-mouth disease caused the REMIDS TDP project to be relocated at Llanbedr which, as Joanna Sale of QinetiQ reported, 'proved to be an excellent site, with great facilities, a unique coastal location and strong support from the local staff. Some 750 inert land mine replicas were deployed in a variety of configurations and test cells over a grassed area of about two square kilometres within the airfield boundary.'

In May Bethan Jones (Admin Manager) and Pauline Wilcox (Manager's Secretary) helped their boss to play an out-of-season 'Father Christmas' for Llanbedr staff who had worked at the airfield since 1st April 1991. The Llanbedr Serco Operations 'Ten Years Service' awards were presented by Contract Manager Paul Whitelegg at a 'buffet and drinks' party on Shell Island.

On 2nd June, Sea Vixen D.3 XP924, now registered to De Havilland Aviation (DHA) as G-CVIX, hit the headlines. The big twin-boomer was flying lead in a two-ship display with DHA's Vampire T.55 U-1234 (G-DHAV) at the 39th Biggin Hill Airshow, when the Vampire appeared to get caught in the slipstream during a turn. As the Sea Vixen pulled away the Vampire spiralled down and crashed, killing the two-man crew of Air Marshal Sir Kenneth Hayr and Jonathan Kerr.

On 19th June George Workman Sr died. Since the beginning of the Second World War he was the owner/operator of Shell

Island, a substantial area of land adjoining the airfield on the seaward side and used intensively by campers during the summer months. Goodwill and collaboration with George and his family were maintained over the years and are expected to continue with his heirs and successors.

From Australia came news of another death, that of Gordon Appleby, Jindivik designer Ian Fleming's draughtsman colleague in 1947/48. Gordon, subsequently an aeronautical designer in his own right, had apparently been living on borrowed time for years. He was supposed to have been on board the prototype Avro Tudor 2 flight that crashed on 23rd August 1947, killing Avro's chief designer Roy Chadwick and test pilot 'Bill' Thorn, but Gordon had fortuitously declined the flight at the last minute when invited to play golf at St Andrews!

In July 'NewDERA' became 'QinetiQ', pronounced 'kin-et-ic', the new name and identity being the 'result of extensive work by the DERA leadership team and their consultants. It is intended to send out the right signals in terms of energy, motion and progress.' The bright blue of the QinetiQ motif was designed to 'capture the positive energy of the company – assertive, inventive and bright' (*DERA News*). With the end of DERA the airfield signs and letterheads had to be changed again and DERA Llanbedr became MoD Llanbedr just in time to welcome the friends and relations of staff to a 'Families Day' in August.

Still in its Luftwaffe camouflage, Alpha Jet ZJ645 taxies out at Llanbedr.

The Hobbs family's contribution to Llanbedr totalled 104 years of service on 8th November when grandson Shaun (25) was presented with his NVQ 3 after six years as an airframe/engine fitter. George had 44 years of service while his wife Margaret had 29 years in charge of the Technical Library; son Kevin's total was 25. 'I'm about ready to phase out,' said George, who continued for a few months as a part-time consultant while his successor Howard Peart familiarised himself with the job. An ex-RAF Engineering Officer, Howard was confident about the future of Llanbedr airfield because: 'The local community is involved, it would be politically short-sighted not to preserve the airfield and there is too much history here.' Howard, born in South Wales, enjoyed running in the local area once he, his wife Pat and their three children had settled in. Howard has run most major marathons and held the RAF Veterans Marathon Title in 1992.

RAF Valley continued to use Llanbedr at every opportunity for their Hawk pilot training and totalled 5,668 movements before and after UAV sorties by the end of the year. Llanbedr also accommodated 14 emergency diversions of Valley-based Hawks.

Reviewing the Llanbedr aircraft at the end of the year, OC Flying Jon Webb said: 'We retain two Canberras in the Stiletto Supersonic Target role. Sadly, the Meteor is approaching the end of its fatigue life so its function will be replaced by enhancing the Jindivik simulator facility at a much-reduced cost. The Alpha Jet, which handles beautifully, is used as Jindivik shepherd to and from Cardigan Bay range and as a videochase air-

craft for air-to-air missile firings. Seven years after we flew Jindivik from Benbecula Airport to examine the feasibility of extending our operation to include the Hebrides range, the possibility of operating Jindivik there to provide a target service for the new generation of air-to-air missiles remains with us today.'

2002

The year began with 33 Jindiviks in stock (15 of the 800 series and 18 of the 900 series) and Serco continued to operate the airfield under MoD contract. Already on the year's programme was the provision of Jindivik targets by day (and occasionally by night) for over a dozen air defence, ground attack and support squadrons of the RAF and Royal Navy for Tornadoes, Sea Harriers, Harriers and Jaguars. Eurofighter 2000 Trials in Cardigan Bay were also supported by Llanbedr.

As always, a variety of helicopters were accommodated. Most frequent visitors were Army Air Corps helicopters from Middle Wallop in Hampshire, on detachment for pilot training; also Sikorsky MH-53M 'Pave Low IIIs' from the 21st SOS, US Air Force based at RAF Mildenhall in Suffolk. Llanbedr also welcomed AAC Lynx on outboard machine gun development trials, AAC Apache AH.1 attack helicopters on refuelling and familiarisation visits, and RAF Chinooks for technical and refuelling purposes. The SAR Sea King HAR.3s of 22 Squadron and the North Wales Police helicopter used the airfield frequently and ATC provided radar cloudbreak procedures for military aircraft returning to base at low level, such as Hawk T.1s and Tornado F.3s from RAF Leeming in Yorkshire.

In March came the announcement that Serco's contract was to be cancelled and Llanbedr would be 'insourced' from 2nd July. QinetiQ, now the MoD-owned science and technology research organisation, was negotiating with the MoD for a long-term contract covering the management and operation of the ranges. It was to operate from an office in London and have two principal sites at Farnborough in Hampshire and Malvern in Worcestershire. QinetiQ had split from DERA, which had metamorphosed into the Defence Science and Technology Laboratory (DSTL) embracing Chemical and Biological Defence, Defence Analysis, Defence Radiological Protection and Defence Research Information. More new signs and letterheads! Market conditions had made it impossible for the British government to carry out the hoped-for stock market flotation.

In May the death of a young man from the village of Llanbedr in a car accident and the serious injuries to his fiancee highlighted the campaign by bereaved relatives and Airfield Operations Officer Tony Townshend for a civilian air ambulance to serve North and Mid-Wales. Delays and difficulties were common in transporting casualties distances of 50 miles or more to hospital when there were large volumes of holiday traffic on the one and only road in and out of the region. 'Donations of well over £2,000 from mourners started off our appeal fund because the Swansea-based Welsh Air Ambulance has yet to be seen north of Aberystwyth,' said Tony. 'It has been handling about 35 call-outs per month while the UK's average call-out for airborne assiatnce from each air ambulance was three times per day. So there is an urgent need for North and Mid-Wales to have its own air ambulance and it could be based here at Llanbedr. We have begun fund-raising projects and a small contribution from everyone would soon make it possible.'

In May QinetiQ launched a US subsidiary to seek new opportunities in the US defence world, and NASA trialled new collision-avoidance systems for UAVs. In the UK the Royal Aeronautical Society's Air Power Group counselled that the need for UAVs to counter surface-to-air threats and in the information field should be among the UK's defence priorities. The priorities were identified as ensuring freedom to operate, gaining and maintaining air superiority and in the area of information superiority.

At the beginning of July the Llanbedr workforce again faced an overnight change of employer, from Serco to QinetiQ, but were relieved that there were no redundancies on this occasion. Once again the signs and letterheads were changed! However, three weeks later, the staff, local residents and businesses were shocked and dismayed by the MoD announcement that the airfield is to be closed in June 2004. The 25-year contract to be signed with QinetiQ in September 2002 was to be based upon what a *QinetiQ News* release described as 'a rationalised range structure providing a more robust and viable business and potentially saving in excess of £30 million'. Under-Secretary of State for Defence, Lewis Moonie said: 'A sad but necessary outcome of this rationalisation plan for the MoD ranges is the requirement for redundancies. However, the signing of the 25-years partnering contract will provide the most sustainable basis for the future of the Test and Evaluation business and encourage further investment.'

A QinetiQ spokesperson told me that the fate of Llanbedr was sealed some years ago by the MoD's decision to compete for target services. QinetiQ took a commericial decision that the previous style of subcontract no longer served a useful purpose and exercised the right to terminate the Llanbedr contract with Serco. There was a trend to move away from Cardigan Bay because of the larger safety traces required by modern aircraft and guided weapons. 'The use of Llanbedr for tactical UAV development/operations has been discussed by the national press but there is as yet no customer willing to bear the costs of the airfield for such purposes. QinetiQ would very much welcome such use and would be delighted to be involved,' I was told.

'It is foreseen that it is not only the families whose main breadwinners work on the site but the closure will have a knock-on effect

'When I drive along the coast road...'

on all aspects of the area's economy' reported the *Cambrian News* on 1 August. Local politicians were dismayed that 'the news was disgracefully sneaked out last week at a final House of Commons session before Parliament's summer recess, which means the the matter cannot be raised again until October' and that the Welsh Assembly denied their request for a recall following the news that 164 jobs would be lost in Meirion-nydd, reported the *Cambrian News*.

Manager Paul Whitelegg said: 'With UAVs at the forefront of military thinking, we are hopeful that the announcement of the closure of Llanbedr is premature. We have plenty of people with UAV experience here. Meanwhile, we'll continue the Jindivik service until Mirach is ready.' The Meteor Mirach is a proven aerial target system that was developed under a 1995 Italian MoD contract for an advanced threat-representative target system. Smaller and cheaper than Jindivik, it is also recoverable. Roger Q Davies, Air Targets Facilities Manager at Llanbedr, said: 'The planned closure is very sad news. However, Llanbedr airfield is a vaulable asset and has so much potential that it will surely have a future.'

When I drive along the coast road between mountains and sea that overlooks Llanbedr airfield and see the two windsocks streaming in opposite directions or pointing towards each other (an occasional phenomenon supposedly peculiar to very few airfields in the world – one of which is in Iraq!), I also hope that the closure announcement is premature, that the airfield has a future and that I shall have cause to revise and update this book many times.

Bibliography

The Sky and I: Veronica Volkersz; W H Allen, 1956.

Golden Wings: Alison King; C Arthur Pearson Ltd, 1958.

RAF Llanbedr: David Annand; David Annand, 1983.

322 Squadron: Drs W H Lutgert, photos by Bart Sorgedrager; Sectie Luchtmachthistorie van de Staf de Bevelhebber der Luchtstrijdkrachten, 1993.

Early Aviation in North Wales: Roy Sloan; Gwasg Carreg Gwalch, 1989.

Wings of War over Gwynedd: Roy Sloan; Gwasg Carreg Gwalch, 1991.

Aircraft Crashes: Roy Sloan; Gwasg Carreg Gwalch, 1994.

No Landing Place: Edward Doylerush; Midland Counties Publications, 1985.

Fallen Eagles: Edward Doylerush; Midland Counties Publications, 1990.

Action Stations 3: David J Smith; Patrick Stephens Ltd, 1981.

Down in Wales: Terence R Hill; Gwasg Carreg Gwalch, 1994.

Down in Wales 2: Terence R Hill; Gwasg Carreg Gwalch, 1996.

Brassey's Unmanned Aircraft: Arthur Reed; Brassey's Publications, 1979.

Testing Colours: Adrian M Balch; Airlife Publications, 1993.

Forever Farnborough: Peter J Cooper; Hikoki Publications, 1996.

Fire Across the Desert: Peter Morton; Australian Government Pubs, 1989.

Blast the Bush: Len Beadell; Weldon Publishing, 1967.

The Legend of Llandwrog: Edward Doylerush; Midland Counties Pubs, 1964.

In Cobhams' Company: Colin Cruddas; Cobham plc, 1994.

Jindivik Target: R L Rothenburg; US Naval Missile Center Tech Memo, 1965.

Outline of the History & Development of RAE Llanbedr: I S Dyer; 1973.

Testing Time: John Miles; Neptune Press, 1979.

Thirty Years Later – Jindivik in Retrospect: Ian Fleming; The Sir Lawrence Wackett Lecture, 1977.

The Sky's the Limit: Wendy Boase; Osprey Publications, 1979.

No Landing Place, Vol 2: Edward Doylerush; Midland Counties Publications, 1999.

RAF Valley 'In adversis perfugium' (1983 souvenir brochure).

Days of Challenge, Years of Change: History of Pacific Missile Test Center.

Firestreak Weapons System Silver Jubilee – 1983: various authors.

Shorts Aircraft and Missiles 1903-1978: Short Brothers Ltd, Belfast, 1979.

Warplane Wrecks of Interest in Snowdonia: Snowdonia Aviation Historical Society.

Britain in Aerospace: The Society of British Aerospace Companies.

Jindivik Target Aircraft: T P Nichols; World Aerospace Systems.

Jane's All The World's Aircraft.